BORN IN BERKELEY

Follow That Beat/A Memoir of the Sixties

By

Lynn Rogers

BORN IN BERKELEY

Follow That Beat/A Memoir of the Sixties

By
Lynn Rogers

ISBN 10: 0-9711039-1-7
ISBN 13: 978-0-9711039-1-7
Library of Congress Control Number 2001090838

Illustrations by the author. Drawn in the 60s and the present.

© 1984, 1991, 1995, 2011 By Lynn Rogers
First Printing - May 2002
Second Printing - July, 2011
Published by Inkling Press
PO Box 2598
Menlo Park, CA 94026
www.inklingpress.com

To my late brother, David Keith Rogers
May 5, 1955 – November 8, 2004
He too lived through the crazy heartbreak
And underlying Love
That once upon a time
Was our Family

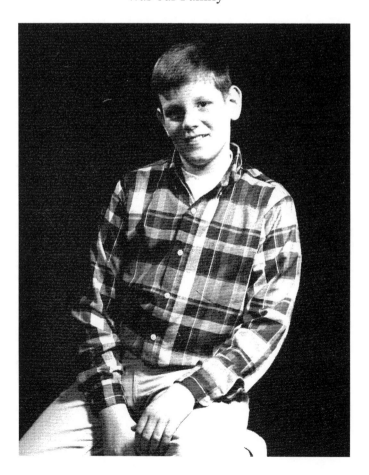

Forward

This is a damned interesting book for a number of reasons. It tells the story of a very young and precocious girl who had the gift of being in some very hip places at the right time. It's a fascinating tour of the west coast hip as it exploded onto the nation's consciousness from the beginning of the Berkeley fight against the Vietnam war to the baths at Esalen, meeting Kesey, Cassady and the Pranksters on the lam in Mexico, in high school with Bob Weir of the Dead, and the communal houses of Palo Alto that touched the Prankster world as well as that of Joan Baez and Ira Sandperl.

What makes <u>Born In Berkeley</u> unique is that it is told principally from the point of view of this young girl. In a sense she's the groupie, standing backstage, just passing through. But she's not starstruck. The famous mean no more to her than the unknowns. And she's a damned good observer of a time when the sexual ethos was a good deal funkier than it is now--an era when some of us were enamored of the cave man style of the Hells Angels and called our lovers our "old lady" or "old man." At 16, Colly knows Neal Cassady is famous but for her he's mostly just a grizzled guy who is a mythic figure to her boyfriends. Most books or movies try to capture the era by retelling the myths of the iconic figures, and she would be just a beautiful young girl who at most rates a name, or "Neal drove up, a gorgeous young girl with him as usual." We lose a lot if we don't hear her perspective at last. It's not one more woman's story of a love affair with a now famous man. It's the story of her love affair with the world and as with any young person, her search for herself.

So for those of us who were there when it seemed a new world was being born, this is a wonderful way to look back through someone else's eyes. And for those of you born too late (you think) or who were for some reason otherwise engaged--don't miss your chance. This is how it was--before there was a Silicon Valley and they paved the whole damned thing.

James Stauffer
Poet, Beat Historian, and co-editor of *"The Fool"*

Although written as a memoir, Caroline Ryder's account of her life and times draws heavily upon the author's life experiences, a time I have come to call the Beat/Hippy Axis.

Chapter One

Born in Berkeley, I grew to my teens in a post-war suburban tract south of San Francisco where the Beats—including the Cassadys, Ginsberg and Kerouac—gathered.

By eleven, I'd roam alone at night out of Tupper's Park, down gray and white streets. It was a neighborhood of sameness. All I'd see above me were pinpricks of stars through the misty white streetlights higher than maples plotted before the tract was conceived.

Tupper's Park in the late fifties and sixties seemed like more of a town than a tract. Being the same was important to my mother. She'd joined the babysitting co-op that spread to most of the families in the park. On the roster she had, were the secrets of its inhabitants.

We were listed as the Ryders, Franklin and Charlene, with Caroline—me, Susan, my younger sister, and my younger brother Keith. I liked to look at the unusual names on the sheet, though.

I didn't feel normal. My mother would yell, "What's wrong with you? Why can't you be like the others?" Even though I was gifted—enriched with audio Spanish tapes in elementary school—Jr. High class valedictorian, captain of the basketball team, lead in the childhood plays, she blamed me for her problems.

From the time we moved to Tupper's Park, she'd keep me up at night, her running through the house threatening to leave my father and us. When I'd huddle at the end of my bed, she'd rush at me and scream, "What's your problem, anyway? You have it good. Nothing like when I was a child on relief." Then she'd start up again.

Once when I was six, we went with my father to Santa Barbara. Working his way up the ladder of the West Coast Interior Department, he had government business there. While he was working, she took us downtown to shop. Suddenly seeing my father and his boss coming up the street at lunch time, she ran off with my brother and sister, to spite him—leaving me alone on the curb.

Thinking she was gone for good, I'd rushed to my father, crying. He'd lifted me up and held me against his good-smelling suit.

"What's wrong with you?" she drilled me later. "You've embarrassed me in front of your father's boss."

No matter what she did to my father and me, she always respected his paycheck and how things looked, to people like the Browns, Jim and Babs, with Tom and Kathy—or the Carlson's, Howard and Eileen, with Pamela, Stephanie and Howard Jr. I liked it when these other parents in the co-op came to sit, because she'd often be punishing me by not speaking to me for days. On those nights, instead of getting up at night to see if she'd forgiven me, I'd find a friendly–faced mom in the living room.

Only none of them knew, or wanted to know, what went on behind the door of our "Leave It To Beaver" house when they weren't there. But somehow I wished they cared. Once when the Brownie troop had the poorest mom pretend to be a gypsy fortuneteller for Halloween, I asked her crystal ball, "Does my mother love me?"

"What's wrong with you, asking that?" my mother demanded later, then didn't speak to me for a long time.

Since I didn't fit in, or didn't want to fit, I liked to think of the Freeman's, Jeff and Natalie, with Hong, Lupita and Gregory. They'd adopted Hong from Korea, Lupita from the Philippines. Then they'd "relaxed", everybody said, and Gregory had come. The Freeman's, Jeff and Natalie, Hong, Lupita and Gregory, had an accessible tree swing in an oak with a cemented hollow. Sometimes I wandered around the corner and slipped into the yard and

2

swung from the branches. It was the only house where a kid whose mother wouldn't speak to her, could visit, and not be looked at, or wondered about, or talked about.

"Did you go to Norine Greene's?" my mother asked one day when I returned from the Freeman's swing. "I'm sure you must have—Norine's a 'nice' girl," she gushed. She so often manipulated shame from me by praising an act she knew I had not performed. I looked down, squeezed in a small space by the shame conjured out of me against my will. "You weren't there," my mother went on. "Then where were you? Not at that house with those foreign children again, not you Caroline, not again. You should play with nice, normal girls. What's the matter with you?"

I skulked into my back room, wondering what was the matter with me. Helpless.

Later that night the table was set. White shiny formica, cold, it caught my dress. I forgot and scraped the gold metal chair on the new white vinyl. Five gold roll-up straw place mats, five dishes waited for the hamburger goulash that simmered on the stove. Tomato, basil, garlic, onion and corn brewed with the meat in the cast frying pan, spewed aromatic steam into the copper hood above the burners.

The telephone rang in the back bedroom. My mother left down the hall, past my sister fighting with my brother Keith.

Coming back from her call, my mother reached for a gray bottle from the bathroom cabinet. She plopped some pills into the pocket of her wrapper, took one out and swallowed it with water. She usually took them later, when she ate the coconut fig cookies no one else was allowed to have—washed down with Orange Pico Tea, or later, too much wine.

That was her time, no one else's. Intruders irritated her.

My younger brother Keith clambered through the kitchen, slung open the sliding glass door, splashed over the rain-wet patio, out to the back grass. Moments later he tamped mud onto the mat, the kitchen floor, dropped his jacket over the chair where it dripped onto the no-wax linoleum. Rain poured from the eaves of the kitchen roof onto the open patio. I slid the glass door shut and locked it.

I was hungry. I opened the refrigerator. The freezer section was stacked with the sandwiches we'd all had to make last Saturday. I could tell which were tuna, which were the peanut butter, or the cream cheese and honey, by the colors of filling stuck to the red waxed paper. She'd said it would save time if we made a month of sandwiches ahead in a batch, but they didn't thaw all the way out by lunchtime, and the bread was still wet and cold. I'd thrown part of mine away at school that day.

Dinner sizzling smelled good. I could hardly wait. She came in, looking sleepier than before, and said "You can wait, Caroline," when I complained, but cooked it faster.

I stacked the whole wheat bread, plopped real butter on a dish to make dinner hurry up. Because there was nothing else to do while she stirred, I presented her the maple leaves I'd found walking home from the Freeman's: red and green, bright black, olive, burnt umber, some had curled leaves.

She said, after dinner, we'd press them beneath the glass top coffee table in the living room with the others I'd brought this week. Babyish, but she liked it. She still liked me to call her Mommy, too. On this night and some others, she made me feel like I was the only one who brought her leaves.

But as I grew older, on mornings after these intimate nights, she threw the breakfast food at me. Years later after they moved out, Keith said he found remnants of hardened eggs and cereal on the backside of the heater. And often, after breakfast she'd pick at imagined blemishes on my face until they bled, and bring me to school late. But after school, she'd be my best friend, inviting me into the bathroom to chat with her where she sat naked. I'd avert my eyes from her massive amber pubic hair.

By nighttime as I grew older, I was the enemy, who kept her awake. At dawn, to punish me, she played radios loud outside my door and later ordered my father to pour water on me to wake me up. Instead, he closed the door and sang corny jingles like, "Good morning, good morning, from Edsel J. Schloss Studebaker," which got me out to the breakfast table where she started all over again.

By sixth grade, if she was mad at me sometimes, while I was at school, she'd dump the contents of my whole room into my bed sheets, tie these in knots, and throw them out into the yard for the school children to see I hadn't cleaned my room. Then she'd take Polaroid pictures of me, wearing ugly glasses she'd bought, snap the shots while I was crying. She threatened to send the pictures to the teacher.

One day, while she was driving us home down the frontage road from my best friend, Abagail Abogada's house, she started in on me again. She stopped the engine in the middle of the road. "It would serve you right if your little friend Abagail knew what you were really like. I have half a mind to drive back there now, and have you tell her—what do you think of that?"

I stared silently at the floorboards of the old '50 Chevrolet, gripping the rounded door handle with white knuckles. She turned to whip me with her car keys. I pushed open the door, jumped out of the car, and fled into the dark recesses of the Flood Tree Preserve. Although I wandered home alone that night, I'd defied her. Things would never be the same. At eleven, in my own way, I was already on the road.

Chapter 2

But I couldn't get away yet. By my early teens I became aware of the barriers that separated our town from the next. Ranch style residences and car dealers obscured boundaries between the suburban towns. Not like when I was small and my mother, into health foods with a vengeance, took us to pick apricots in late summer orchards.

Now my grim parents would shuttle us in the new avocado, 60's wagon, up and down El Camino Real on Saturday errands, intruding at times into Palo Alto, to the cheese shop at Town and Country Village, to the optometrist there to fit me with abhorrent wing tipped eyeglasses—"How could you lose another pair, Caroline?"

Maybe it was these accumulated years watching that sign, "Entering Palo Alto," that did it. Despite being with them, I sensed I had violated a veil, there was a different psychic terrain behind that marker. I hoped there was another world in Palo Alto hidden underneath the cheese shop.

But the new world remained hidden.

I didn't hear more about Palo Alto, until my first year of high school in wealthy Atherton on the Menlo Park border. Young for my class, only a few weeks into it, and President Kennedy was shot.

What ever had been at that school, shifted. Or maybe it was only me. During that stage I tried everything, trying to belong somewhere after being cast out, or casting myself out of the clique I'd been bred to join. From Jr. High Valedictorian to cotillion dance lessons, the way should have been clear. But the problems with my mother and my own nature meant I wasn't going to make it in the snobbish, materialistic, racist high school circle. I was going another way.

At 14, I flitted through the personas of Presbyterian Youth group member, surfer, acting student, greaser's bad girl.

At the end of that year I'd taken to wandering under moonlight with Mak, the poet kid in the house behind. A muscular Irish Catholic senior whose dad hated him, Mak acted in avant-garde little theatre, played a muscled Mexican in Tennessee Williams' *Night of the Iguana* there. I hung out behind the scenery with him, ushered, and wrote poetry and dialogue. That is on the nights we weren't wandering out of Tupper's Park by moonlight, or surfing illegally in the Tree Preserve pool.

Then I'd haul myself out the window, catch the wild whiff of adventure the second my head was through the jam. He'd grin and whisper, "Pss-sst".

"Shhh—", I'd intone, but he never would be quiet. I'd lower myself to the ground with an ankle-testing thud. We'd weave around the garbage cans, finger the gate with cat's paw hands, return to shut it, we were off.

By one A.M. we'd have been in the James Flood Tree Preserve for hours and I'd say we should sneak home. But Mak's wet, triumphant grin told me we wouldn't go back until much later.

If it was a typical night, we'd scaled the wall of the fenced-off Flood pool with two of his neighborhood friends and their surf-boards. The guys made waves for us kicking up the dark water at the other side of the pool. Mak and I knelt on boards and scooped at the shallow waves to build momentum. It would be our turn to make the waves until the security guard's flashlight dipped up and down amongst the trees outside, and we all would be quiet, still bodies and boards beneath the deep end waters, like sleeping fish in the Fleischacker Aquarium after dark.

With Mak too, I made it to the Berkeley Greek theatre once for a folk concert, him walking on the other side of the street because we both thought I looked stupid in the harlequin glasses and sweater my mother had picked out for the trip. OK for us to stay overnight in Oakland with my aunt.

That year, on my own, I ventured out as far as poorer Redwood City too, and richer Atherton, where an older student, overdeveloped, wealthy Letty Underwire, invited me on my first double date at her parents' emptied mansion.

I watched Letty's bosom groped by slim, cashmered Stanford University boys; I was jackknifed for an uncomfortable evening in some guy's lap. Letty Underwire had a girlfriend, Emma C. Smith, equally buxom, also older than me, who wore sweaters, who'd chosen sex as part of her visible personae too, but there the resemblance stopped.

Emma's eccentric parents lived in the part of lower white Menlo Park that pushed against East Palo Alto. Instead of voting for Nixon like my parents, they'd been driven here from back east, Emma'd said, labeled communists, and pinko Jews.

Her brother had been at the University of California–Berkeley. The family worried about him, said he'd had a breakdown. Skinny and ragged-bearded, he was the antithesis of Emma. Though both had high IQs like me, she embodied her flesh, made friends through her pointed-bra, then later–no-bra, chest. At seventeen, Emma was a woman and at fifteen and the beginning of the sophomore year I was a girl.

Emma told me about Quaker meetings in Palo Alto, where I heard longhaired young students sing folk songs about peace. They needed fund-raisers to help Negroes vote down south. Having been trod on by my mother, I identified with the Negroes' plight right away.

The Student Non-Violent Coordinating Committee appealed to me. Hovering between religion and rebellion, I'd found an answer—a way of doing something good for those on the fringes of society.

 S.N.C.C. raised money for civil rights workers in the south. We learned Negro voting rights activist James Meredith was wounded by gunfire on a Mississippi highway. And how a worker from Mississippi gave a speech at the University my parents had attended. U.C. Berkeley administrators prevented students from collecting money for such civil rights workers. In a fiery speech Mario Savio said, "There is a time when operation of the machine becomes so odious it makes you sick to heart that you can't take part."

 I joined the committee that first night, and found an identity at once, among the idealistic sons and daughters of Stanford professors more concerned about racial injustice than shopping. A Negro leader from East Palo Alto spotted me as a natural spokesperson for the cause.

 Weeks later, I hitchhiked home from a Presbyterian ski trip, to work at the fund-raiser we'd planned at the American Veteran's hall in Redwood City. I took up the microphone and convinced the World War Two Vets to give their Negro brothers down in Selma, Alabama, a real chance to participate in "our great country you saved from the enemy overseas. You helped free the Jews from the concentration camps. Let's free our Negro brothers and sisters to vote." I was proud of the five hundred dollars that came back in the basket.

 After that, I hopped the bus and rumbled over to Palo Alto every chance I got.

 On Saturday mornings University Avenue was long and mysterious, with the usual posh dress shops like those in Menlo Park, and with supercilious, vacuous saleswomen who seemed to live to look down on one who wore a Veteran's Thrift Shop jacket. They regarded me with disdain, unless they smelled money through the crunchy leather. Then they beckoned me in. It was a game, between these ladies and me, a game of which I soon tired.

 If I went in to buy something, nice, normal, as my mother so often cajoled, I came back out psychically soiled, hiding deeper beneath the natty old collar, buried deeper in the pockets of the man's thrift-shop jacket.

After that, I could walk to upper University—top end of the downtown, before approaching the wide eucalyptus boulevard that led into historic Stanford University, or else I could walk way down lower University, to Whiskey Gulch at the beginning of the one mile limit from Stanford. Beyond that, University Avenue crossed the freeway and deepened, meandering into East Palo Alto—the Negro ghetto, the other, subliminal, inner, side of the city. There, those things repressed, disdained by the lady shopkeepers at Weideman's and the other swank stores, lived.

But in between University and ghetto, hidden in fine interstices between the classic foreboding shops and the normalcies my mother loved, were hidden caches of life: I didn't know many yet, but enough to make me wander out of Menlo Park and look.

Palo Alto, 1965

I sprang up High Street in the early afternoon, pushing straight light brown hair out of my face and over my shoulders. I wore a striped blue and crimson man's sweater, orange brown moccasins, and my setter-brown jacket. I slipped my hands down dark Levis, and sauntered along.

It was about 3:30. The streets were white in the winter sun. Picturesque frame houses lined the narrow street I turned onto, some houses were more run-down and overgrown than others. Nothing like this in our tract. Today I'd see a house I liked, smile, but didn't miss my stride.

At High and Addison I glimpsed ahead, a glassed-in porch. Easels standing inside, supporting bright, free abstract paintings. I loped from the sidewalk across the grass and up the steps to a house I'd never seen before. I pulled at the door handle, shouted "haloo" several times.

No answer. I stepped into the bright-lit porch room and walked between the easels, not minding the papers spread on the floor with the still-wet paint splotches on them. I breathed deeply and long, bent over the easels reverently, breathing again. The smell

11

of tacky paint, the banana-bright dream colors on one, the wishful runny blue purple obscuring the slight outline of a stooping nude on the second, the laughing, fall reds and emerald green merging in the last, made me call out again.

No one around still. But I left with a wild free hunger for the art.

That hunger brought me to the Palo Alto border again and again. I'd start at Kepler's books on El Camino with its thick coffee and baklava, with the beat books—Ginsberg's *Howl*, Ferlinghetti's *Her*, Patchen's *Love Poems*—bought one from peace advocate Ira Sandpearl. From this I discovered St. Michael's Alley in Palo Alto, the hipster's restaurant with Sandpearl and his pal Joan Baez among the regulars. St. Michael's Alley. With talk of Lyndon Baines Johnson's recent innaugeration and Martin Luther King's Civil Rights demonstrations.

I dug the long narrow coffee shop and restaurant on University Avenue, beer kegs and Haitian dealers lurking in the back, blackboard with specials served with big ruffled purple cabbage leaf garnishes—and the jukebox with jazz. From these encounters I learned Baez had helped set up the counter culture Pacific High School.

Persuaded I might better use my creativity there, my mother who'd liked my drawings and pressed leaves as a child, had let me attend. More and more disconnected from Atherton High School, I was glad to be in the class just after the Grateful Dead's Bob Weir. Students took a bus way up Skyline Boulevard to Pacific High School, clambered down a hillside and read T.S. Eliot in the rain, and tried abstract painting.

From this inspiration I also persuaded my mother to let me have $25.00 for half the rent of an occasional use Palo Alto "artist's studio" I'd share with an older girl from Pacific—really a room with cracked linoleum floors and a gas-leaking kitchen on Everett Street. On our first artistic evening, we meandered over to St. Michael's Alley.

After awhile, the girl went home. I wasn't ready yet, I was never ready to go home. Some older twenty-something, short guy in a cowboy hat wanted to show me his "etchings". Never having heard the expression before, and wanting to be cool with these older, artistic individuals, I followed him to a pad, ran around in circles to get away from him, and came back.

Later, some jazz aficionados let me come along with them to a rambling Palo Alto Victorian. Some gal heated me a bowl of Campbell's soup, people cleared out after midnight, someone gave me a sleeping bag. I woke up before dawn when a jazz musician came in from his all night gig. We sat talking in his room. Out the window by first light I began to see men in trench coats. Then came hard knocks. It was the FBI, tracking some guy from Virginia on a marijuana charge. Glad to find a fifteen-year-old girl in the house, they dumped my purse on the table, were sure my new eyeliner cake was dope. One of the men tasted the eyeliner cake, eager for evidence of contraband. Sorely disappointed to find out it was from Walgreen's, they called my parents and hauled me away anyway.

I spent three days at Hillview Juvenile facility where they tested me for evidence of sexual relations with the marijuana suspects–again finding nothing. My mother's generosity understandably turned, she told them all my faults—I wouldn't make the bed, whatever she could think of–which led them to the idea I might be incorrigible. It was cinched, when the matron caught me reading a supportive note from a Negro male student friend from Pacific High. For this worst of all offences, she recommended three years incarceration at the Youth Authority. At the last minute my father's lawyer, Abagail Abogada's dad, intervened, and I was released from the hearing room.

Perhaps I was incorrigible. By the time I was well into fifteen, I was spending more and more time away from home.

Chapter 3

Big Sur, 1965

The car turned off Highway One, the old road running the length of California. Seventy miles below Monterey it chugged, braked, down a narrow unpaved road along a steep cliff above the sea. Something, a sweet smell—a weed?—wove back at me through the open window. I felt a male knee jostling against mine. I clung to the inside door handle, glad I was on the highway side, and could not see all the way down.

I was in the back seat with some boy I knew from my new progressive School my parents paid for when I couldn't hack Menlo Atherton High School any more. Sponsors like Joan Baez and Ira Sandperl, musical students from Bob Weir just ahead to Negro kids on scholarship from the Fillmore, Keplers and the Quakers had prepared me for this. Self- educated before, I read all the time.

The boy's friend Carl drove. Next to him through his girl-friend Starla's open front passenger side window, I could see the wide eye of the moon. I sucked in the scent of cold sweet weeds, even reached my finger out into the fog.

The car rose, bobbed, swam slowly, headlights lifting up each clump of weeds we passed, bringing them into view. My back seat companion Jeff laid his arm lightly around my neck; his hand dangled down my side. I shimmied closer to him.

The car dove into a pothole.

"Want some of this, little one?" Starla laughed.

"What is it?" I heard a voice like a squeeze coming out of me.

"Weed. Grass, dummy," she said. "Mari juana—Mary whoana," Carl joined in.

"Here, baby, take it," Jeff commanded.

Contrary to the FBI's suspicions, I didn't even smoke. I pursed my lips. Jeff stuffed the fat cigarette into my mouth. I breathed deep, with my mouth, nose, all at the same time—I got a little, mostly fresh air.

"I'm not sure I want it, Jeff," I said. "Someone told me it does bad things to you."

"Then don't, child." He withdrew his hand, gentle padded fingers dragged back across my collar.

"I want you," he murmured, but in a way that sounded a little mean.

"Just a minute more and we'll make it, man." Starla's guy Carl steered the car like one of the buoys or dinghies we'd seen floating off the pier that afternoon passing Monterey Bay.

"We're sailing now." They all laughed—all three, and sailed down about five more potholes, and then veered to the left and an uneasy stop.

"To the baths!"

"To the baths!"

The others sprang out with the towels Jeff had packed earlier, in hand. I followed them down a dark narrow path. The sea glimmered to their right, below a ragged cliffside. One dim light dared us to approach a low shadowy structure. A naked man with a grin like a Jack O' Lantern leapt out of nowhere.

My heart beat harder. I tried to stop my feet from running

16

down—not easy when the road carried me quickly. I backed away from Jeff, into the hillside. The dewy brush of weeds against a little uncovered place on my ankle stilled the fear. The man passed.

At least the wet grass was fresh and real. Jeff held my hand tightly. We clambered down.

The stone structure received us. Inside it was gray, lit very dimly by candles interspaced in what appeared to be a labyrinth, a catacomb.

I thought of the early Christians, about the martyr boy I'd read about in Presbyterian Sunday school.

I followed Carl and Starla and then Jeff, down narrow steps between stone walls, around a dark corner, then down another set of steps, and then—we stepped out onto a wet floor in a three-sided building that sheltered two huge, dark stone baths before a ghostly veranda railing, and then a sheer drop to the sea.

Jeff walked to the railing, waved for me to join him. Together we watched the moonlit, iridescent waves crash the rocks beneath. I looked behind me, heard the subtlest splash in the tub. Carl and Starla were already taking off their clothes. Starla bent, shadowy breasts dipping long in the semi-dark. Fog and strange mists imbued my lungs.

I watched Jeff strip, and I followed suit. He stepped over the stone ledge and disappeared deep into the smaller of the two tubs. First his legs receded, then the dark member at his groin beneath his wide, white trunk. I saw at last his head above the water and then his wet hands making wide playful gestures for me to follow.

I dropped everything on one of the benches that lay before the ledge of the Deep Drop. Then, teats hard and wizened from the cold, bare buttocks and back feeling the whispery wind, I slid over to him, stepped high over the stone side that formed a seat, sat on the coarse slab, until, goosebumped everywhere, I sank into the hottest water I'd ever felt. I lowered myself slowly, clutching the pebble protrusions of the wall behind me for safety.

I slowly floated down, buried by sulfur water. Then before I could assimilate this, his foot poked at me, my thigh was grazing

17

his, back and forth.

"This is beautiful, Jeff."

He grabbed at me. My breasts were floating, the nipples made crests of flesh waves. He put his arms around my back and pulled me closer.

His thing was wet, rubbery, wide and stiff. It pricked the inside of my thigh in its wide swing—side to side. I could feel a ridge at the end of it. He was rubbing it against me. He didn't seem able to stop.

I moved away, spread my legs wide, sitting—but I floated—bent my head in the water, outstretched my hands. I surrendered to the water. But my newformed breasts still floated. I coiled like a fetus and bobbed away to the corner, far from Jeff.

"Let's get out of here, Colly, I'm too hot."

I stood and Jeff stood. His Minotaur's shadow covered the back wall of the building away from the sea. He took my hand, walked me back the way we'd come, to the right and down more steps, to the left and suddenly we were alone in another similar rock rook. The three-sided empty bathhouse opened to the overwhelming sound of the sea.

I looked at him. Why were we here? Did he want to try these baths instead?

He led me to a bench at the far end of an open porch and pushed me, butt up like a boy on the wooden planks. I imagined I lay like a girl lying in flowers on a bright summer's day. And then I realized, he wanted to make me. Detached, I savored the new word.

He wants to ball me, I said to myself. This Big Sur was 1930s epic sex author Henry Miller's country. We all aspired and adopted to talk like Miller's books. He turned me over. He pushed my legs apart until they hung down off either side of the bench. He rose above me.

It aimed, a gray rubber missile I thought, somewhere out of view—down lower on my body. A pad of hair on his chest scratched my chest. He lowered his breath in my ear, his tongue wet, rubbery, warm, traced the seashell inside ridges of my ear,

18

obscuring the pounding crashing sea sound beneath. In his breath I heard another rise, tension and crash.

"Are you a virgin?"

"I'm a virgin." You had to lie but how much of a lie was it? After a pretty chaste relationship for nine months with the Presbyterian youth boy, I'd tried something one night late at my parent's house, but he couldn't go very far, and I didn't feel anything.

I tightened, got cold all over, tightened with the lie to please. When Jeff put it in it was tight. It stung, so it was not all a lie. That one other time—that dim, almost-in, Church youth group trip aftermath, that other Jimmy-Sunday school time, did not count.

Tonight it fed into me and stopped, then, thrill! He made his tongue stop me listening to my lying, fed tongue warmth into me at the same time he fed in a wide octopus head; and his arms were all around me, his legs between my knees, entangling around me.

I arched on the hard bench, heard the heightened fluorescent sea raining down over conch shells, felt the world's heart sinking down the drain of the sea which engorged and fed the morass of shells, heard the cacophony of fishes and weeds and undersea terrain—and human beings, all sliding down its deep great drain.

After seconds, quiet. His breath blubbered on me. As he breathed, the hair mat swished back and forth across my chest.

I felt slippery against him—my hand and forearms grew cold. Still, he breathed like dead. Though quiet and inert, somehow not a weight, he was a heavy flesh blanket to warm me, press my ribs and heart up against on this bench. My mind remained free.

Now I wasn't a girl, but an incipient woman. An intriguing experience, but one sided, and somehow years of being told to be a nice polite girl had gotten to—even—me. I lay there under him without complaint, until some inside part of me popped out beyond bones and adolescent flashes and two old minds. I had a vision I couldn't remember right after, but I knew I'd had it, like life unconsciously expressing itself before it could be named.

And, following them up the hillside later I realized that, although afraid at moments, I'd been cool tonight, and for me in those times, to be cool was all.

So cool, that the next time I got back to Big Sur during Easter vacation week, I followed a group of hip college students over a no trespassing sign onto a deserted beach to make fires 'till the dawn. Sometime in the night the police came through our trail in the grass and led us to their paddy wagons.

After the Hillview fiasco, I knew better than to say I was a juvenile when they arrested us for trespassing. On the drive to the jail I fished my I.D. out of my bag and ate it. It separated into pieces and tasted like gluey gum. The last chunk was hard to swallow.

This incarceration turned out to be fun. I made up an alternate identity—an Irish surname, birth city of San Francisco and an earlier birth date. At the Monterey County adult jail, a person got to stay with their friends, have cigarettes if they smoked, and make phone calls.

People sang, and derided the police. It was all going well until my alternate birth data didn't check out. They sent me home on a bus. I was disappointed.

Big Sur

Weeks later, ocean breaking on the cliffs at Esalen. I had gotten a ride back here with Letty Underwire—she'd gone off with the Gypsy Jokers Biker's Club. At the gas station where the ride stopped, the bikers asked me to come along too, but something, the way they revved their motors, something inside said no. On the outskirts of Esalen's land I wandered into a thatched cliffside cottage. A Mimi and Dick Ferina record played. A loom—I gathered in impressions—a bowl of gruel.

A woman. Two men. In whispers like monks and nun.

And another young man in a big coat read a poem from a scrap of paper. In awe, I turned slowly, saw the woman, hand long and sinewy, stir water in a small metal pot set on a wide black burner. A foghorn squeezed out all other sounds, rolled in—and out. Its low tones submerged the Big Sur coast.

I put down my thrift shop man's orange leather jacket, fingered my long hair falling in front of my face. In the light of the crackling fire beneath the wood burner, it dripped white, yellow, amber and brown.

The young scrap man, like a white shadow, clung to his paper after the reading. He looked, grabbed me with his gaze. I followed him with mine. Without a sound we left, my leather fringe jacket trailing behind me, away from the one room that glowed on its briar promontory hidden above the swift drop over the cliff to the sea.

The man was young and fair in his neither brown nor yellow hair but clear light dun, like the down of thistles that bloomed around on the cliff top. He led me through the dark, around the edge of briars, then thickets, and then deep into a wood. By some agreement, we never spoke, but walked and walked among deep ferns, snapping twigs on needles over loam beneath. As we got deeper into the forest, wide sentinel redwood trees presided, trees that had been here since before we were born this time.

Into a long wind of very dark wood, lit with his dim flashlight we wove. I followed him, padding over mound rises and between stones I knew marked a way. I stepped in moccasin feet until we stopped to cross beneath a waterfall. Standing close, me behind him not touching, a rock wall on the left, a water curtain on the right, like long lonely hair through which I could see moonlight in the clearing about the fall, playing rainbow prisms in deep dark.

When we arrived at the place where the trail made a loop, we lay on a slightly raised ledge dug against the mountaintop.

He laid my jacket beneath my head, unrolled a bag out on swept-over needles, and nestled beside me on the loam. Without the light, I could not see his face. Without more age I could not come with a man, I let him into me like his poem, pinned cold between soft giving loam and he who did not speak. I listened to the distant sound of sea and loam, thought I heard Mimi and Dick intermingling on dulcimers in deepest woods.

Before dawn he cradled my face, got up, made a sort of soup with noodles, yellow like his part flaxen hair. We didn't look into each other, or ask about anything. He rolled up his bag and led me out the way we'd come. I followed him, like a novitiate behind a hair-breath older monk, followed his lead, unraveled the rite that had led us in, left as if over the deep rug of a Cathedral.

Once out he took me back among his friends of the previous night. As we approached, they were gathering with others in the half-light outside the house, where speckled granite slabs made seats for each one of them. The two men and the woman leaned in these berths and watched the earth release a wan amber moon—it was a wisp, a girl. In awe we embraced the coming of the wide bosom of sky, then through pouty cloud lips, the core white clit of sun. Like a woman's heat it warmed the wet ground on which we stood and dried it.

I took the fifth stone. Before I sank down, long legs outstretched, feet free over the steep cliff's edge, I reached out my arms and widened my hands, one toward the young man's chest, where I did not feel it touch, the other toward the empty stone to my right.

They pulled on something like cigarettes. Must be marijuana. A subtle smell riveleted to me, then was blown away, down the path. They had begun to talk, two men in rumbled hornlike, low voices, the woman on my left bending against the dampened chest of a man with reddish bramble beard. She murmured and stroked her fingers over his reddish skin glistening in the light of the sunrise.

"What's her name?" the man two slabs down asked the youth beside me, in a voice that surfaced just above the crack of waves on rock, and the foghorn.

Last night's woodsman pulled at his strange cigarette between his lips, holding his breath in a long silence. He gestured toward me. "Girl," he named me.

Girl, I thought. And all at once I was girl, the first girl, the only girl in creation, and not a girl at all, but an idea, an essence.

I stood up straight, walked to the cliff's edge, my toes curling the moccasin leather down over the edge. "Girl" breathed in the morning's first sun, saw white light spattered back at her eyes from over blue ocean waves, and knew it was good.

Chapter 4

I, Girl, wrote poems in the car now. As my father drove the hapless five of us, drove back and forth across the marshes toward the Dumbarton Bridge crossing the southern end of the San Francisco Bay, I looked for beauty.

The colors that came to my pen were grays, the beauty, the beauty of sticks. Riding in the far back, I felt sick from the rumbling swirl of the moss-colored station wagon. The clicking of my mother's teeth, the in sucking of my mother's tranquilized breath, made me gasp for fresh air and find none. The car cloyed at me, the impassive, cold faces of my brother and sister talking about a police car passing, whether they'd "get" the marsh artists, the scrungy bohemians who converged here, also made me sick.

"Roll the window down, Dad, could you?" I asked.

He looked back at me in the rear view mirror. Eyes hardened to hazelgray nuts, creased mouth etching out a smile for the younger children's "normal" conversation, he deigned to open the window an inch and a half. Our early closeness had been eclipsed by my mother's constant anger, and by his sense that my adventures violated his beliefs.

I didn't want to face disappointing him again. Rolling along I thought of the fog, of the loom, the loam, the woman and the red-bearded man, the wood boy, the rising sun...but these thoughts only came to fill the interstices between my mother's clenched teeth, her nervous lips pursing, "Watch out," my father's bitter hatred, and my siblings' derision. It all made me sick.

As we got nearer the Dumbarton Bridge, we first passed the dump, where the pungent odor of waste rose up to meet us between carcasses of rusted-out cars and strewn debris. I hunched forward over my notebook, clasping at last, this slight swell of beauty, to pen.

Eight weeks later I tacked a note to the kitchen bulletin board, swung my knapsack over my shoulders and left by the back door. I'd had enough of this. They would read the note and think I'd gone camping with my Pacific High School friend, Olive Schreibner.

I circled my birthday on the three-year calendar on the same bulletin board. Three years from now—really only two and a half, I'd be 18 and out of here. Night after night, I'd stood behind the door to my "mother's" room while she'd raved and screamed and torn into me—silently swearing, one day I would never come back. Maybe I thought this would be it, I didn't know. I just had to be free.

The Joan Baez concert would be held at Esalen this vacation week 1965. Baez' sister Mimi Farina would appear along with Mimi's husband Dick—and folksingers Malvina Reynolds and Pete Seeger.

When the bus pulled into Monterey, a feeling like hunger swept over me. After that, it would be a short bus ride, and then a long hitchhike, to the Esalen baths and grounds. By now I knew from Olive, Esalen held therapy conferences with the famous Fritz Perls. With my leather fringe jacket, straight hair, jeans and moccasins, I hoped I looked older than 15.

At home I'd felt 100 years old. Rumbling down the coast, let abhorrent home images flee by. Kids I'd been friends with since elementary school asking—why are you so tired? Don't you sleep? They didn't know what it was like, staying up till two each night, the only time it was peaceful and alone.

They didn't know how much I needed the peaceful time away from the screaming, my mother chasing me through the house yelling "You're insane, not normal, should be locked up." That, or mocking in a sugar-sweet, taunting voice, "You need a psychiatrist."

In a fit of temper, she'd given my room to my younger sister, dumped me by the garage, and moved my sister's things in, while I was at school. And I still smarted from before that, when she'd thrown my possessions out on the lawn, my bedroom furniture and soiled laundry tied in impossibly knotted sheets. I'd been mortified when the boy next door had walked by our low fence and seen the mess.

I'd been even more embarrassed when she'd taken pictures of me in the ugly, pointed harlequin glasses while I sat in the ruin of my room after it was dragged back in, and dumped all around me in a heap. That I'd been crying and my skin was still broken out from her pinching, had added to my humiliation.

For months after that, she'd kept that picture, threatening to send it to school for all my classmates to see if I didn't do what she wanted.

By now, much of my life at home was an ugly secret I kept. When I'd rushed to regular high school, disheveled and late, I'd thought it my fault that, though during junior high I managed to keep grades high and become a valedictorian, by high school, they'd began to slip.

But at Pacific High School there were no grades—only the T.S. Eliot discussions, abstract art, and an anthropology trip—living for a month with the Hopi Indians in Arizona. Our school director had met the Hopi leader David Banyacao when he'd been on the road, years earlier.

The cold desert nights, Kachina dolls and an audience with the elders whose ancient stories about the earth turning over three times before—the end of this century being the pivot time again—would stay with me. But along with a couple of kids from homes like mine, I was stupidly too busy experimenting taking cold pills to change our consciousness, to appreciate the sanctity of the experience. Because of our confused experiment, my pacific experience had been short-lived. As the kid with the least clout and family support, they used me as an example and threw me out.

Back at regular high school again, somehow I couldn't do much homework. I felt like a failure everywhere. I stayed up all night, wrote false excuses, crept back to the attic to catch up on sleep during the day without my mother hunting me down. Secretly ashamed I'd screwed up at cool Pacific High too, I spent more and more time away from school and the kids I'd come up with, especially those in the programs for the gifted.

The only other outcast in my neighborhood was of course Mak—Kelly MacEgan—whose dad seemed jealous of his youth, physical prowess and poise. Only his father railed at him too, constantly berating him in front of all of his friends, and particularly his mother. Mak hungered for the arts like me, and had gotten bits and parts in the local players, Tennessee Williams plays. And by now we'd ranged together beyond the peninsula to Berkeley's Greek Theatre and other spots, listening to Joan Baez' folk concerts there, to walking into North Beach in the San Francisco fog, for City Lights Bookstore, where, despite his father's derision, Mak was later published.

It was heady, exciting relief from the shame and the torment at home. The artistic instincts I'd always had, were nourished in these circles, though no longer in the school where I sat dispirited, day after day. I'd come each morning feeling gritty and unprepared—but acting tough and uncaring toward all the super-bright but still-succeeding girls and boys of my high school advanced-standing classes.

There I would scrunch in an army jacket and salvation tie, worn over the hated, still-mandatory dress or skirt. Once I came early to class after taking Benzedrine for three days—somehow I felt like a success that day—I'd been so wired, I'd read all the bibliography and the footnotes of the history text three times, and managed to score an "A" on a final after this one session on bennies, while not studying all term. Perhaps because the teacher was Negro—from colored to Negro, the current term—I knew I could not fail in his class—not I, who single-handedly raised $500.00 toward voter registration. I couldn't be a failure here.

And the literary magazine published my anti-racial and Big Sur poems, but otherwise, I acted like I didn't care.

"And if you say he'll bring me down..." the racial one started.

Still, there was a price for this—always a price to one's self esteem. The brief moments of success gained this way didn't give me entry back into the fold of my "normal" classmates. Perhaps I was, as my mother screamed so often, sick, crazy, bad. But something in me rebelled against my mother's blame and the pressures and suffering that were home.

On this exciting warming night above the crashing Pacific Ocean, I nestled in my spare sleeping bag on a grassy knoll above the Big Sur cliff. I'd eaten some dried soup, mixed with faucet water in an old camping tin I'd smuggled in the bag. I was afraid, though I wouldn't let it show, even to myself.

In the warmer morning I awakened to find a bearded, bespectacled young man nudging me from where he sat outside the sleeping bag. Confused, I pretended for a moment, still to be asleep. I didn't know who he was or what he was doing—being "cool" was the ultimate here. As he began to stroke my arm that stretched outside the bag and into the damp, bent, cliff grasses, I flinched involuntarily.

I opened my eyes. He stared straight at me and bent to kiss me. I turned away.

"What are you doing?" I asked.

"I'm from U.C. Santa Cruz. I'm doing a study on what would be the reaction of...a...sleeping girl, to a guy's advances."

"Oh." I didn't want to interrupt his study, but this felt awkward and uncomfortable. Besides, I probably looked puffy and ugly, sleeping. I always felt ugly, lately.

My mother said, "You make yourself ugly. Wearing those hideous bohemian styles. No one likes that ugly way of dressing."

I'd kept on dressing that way. Since I was dressing to please myself, to make myself as beautiful as I could in the colors and styles that attracted me, I must be pretty pathetic.

I rolled over, so that he couldn't see my face. He seemed to think I was neat—he said so. "You're O.K."

"Thanks. But I really should get up—get out of here—there will be people coming for the concert." I peeped out at him from under my arm.

"Oh, yeah. People coming." He looked about him as if he were checking to see if someone might be coming. "See you later, O.K.?" He was gone.

I rolled up the thin bag and stuffed it in my knapsack. I ate a banana and a candy bar I'd brought and walked stiffly to the bluff over the ocean.

Blue mist, froth from a thousand nighttime breakers, hung about the rocks. Everywhere below me over and past the rocks were tones of blinding blue and white. Even the sun, though faintly yellow, was pressing through bright white clouds over a wide expanse of muddy indigo and cerulean blue sky.

Cerulean. I'd memorized that word on one of my vocabulary jags. Although I'd been pretending to ignore school, I ate words almost sometimes, and studied or thought of one as if it were a powerful inner secret, to say "cerulean", inwardly, alone in the school library where I'd hidden out. Avoiding only getting a B or a C on a test I hadn't studied for, I'd clasped the warm word "cerulean" like the forgiving hand of a bright friend.

Now I scrunched on the top of the embankment above the dangerous drop to the cliff, and wrote "cerulean" in a dull pencil stroke on the outside of a wadded-up paper bag from my pocket. A tumble of white and blue-silver words followed, streaked out on the bag in the livid lead of the pencil.

Satisfied, I clambered back up from the very edge of the cliff to the grassy knoll and headed toward the Esalen lodge to watch the influx of early arrivals to the Baez concert.

Beaded youth, young men and women from all over California, streamed down around a radiant, God's eye-shaped swimming pool below the rustic lodge and above the breathtaking Big Sur sea.

Those who had "crashed" along the road in redwoods, or, like me, who'd slept in isolated patches of Esalen grasses, were the first to emerge. Joining them were flute-playing, sandaled youths with bells and Eucalyptus bead necklaces and red Indian saris and hash and reefers and girlfriends and boyfriends and occasionally a baby, or dog. A sense of excitement, responsibility, and purity of heart flowed with them. They clotted the knoll at Esalen before the concert began.

And then, bursting from a shiny, purple-black, narrow sports car, came Baez, the magnificent, the Queen. She was the Lady, the legend of the hour. Before Baez played her guitar and sang, the dulcimer tones of Baez's sister Mimi and Mimi's husband Dick Farina floated over the grounds.

I felt my heart would break. I felt fed, healed, hushed, O.K., beautiful, amid the strains of the dulcimer. The crush and throttle of the now-packed crowds of daring, seeking spirits who came to hear Joan, Malvina, Pete, Mimi and Dick—so young, he would soon be dead—weave the mystery of sea and sky and sunny protest against all cruel wrongdoing, into the celebration of these emerging sixties.

But then I was only a child—or was I?—only an onlooker, too young. No, I felt one hundred years old—good, here. I sucked the sea and sounds until the sun and later fine, rising ocean spray washed me clean enough of all the hurt, so that on blind, happy instinct, I decided, after the concert, I decided, to move up the road with the rush of people and follow them into the future, wherever they might go.

I would not go home, I would hitchhike away, down the road and follow that beat.

Chapter 5

Venice, California

The road rolled out before us, the most beautiful road I had
ever seen. The boy and the man who'd driven me down this coast all
night from Esalen, looked tired, but I was puppy happy. I clutched
the boy—the young guy's hand, his face grayish in the new morning
light, the brown eyes that had sparked the night as he talked about
Zen, were resting. Thor, the man, had driven, big red-haired hands
on either side of the steering wheel—toward Venice.

Thor had driven us all the way through Venice and then
further south to the Midnight Onion Folk Bar on a pier. Getting
out, I overheard Thor murmur to the boy Matthew, "This is Orange
County, be cool with the girl, man."

"Be cool with the girl, man," I repeated to Matthew's tired,
but Zen-untroubled face.

But I was tongue-tied after Thor dropped us off. The happy
warmth subsided. We walked across the parking lot. I heard the
sea, this time diluted by daytime street sounds and distant beach
voices.

"Wait here." Matthew went inside the Midnight Onion, returned almost immediately, with a key. He led me to a Volkswagen bus in the side parking lot. We stepped up through a sliding side door, crawled in over neatly folded blankets, some clothes, reclined along a raised pad.

"I'm sleepy," Matthew murmured gently, then cuddled away from me and dropped off. My head was at the end of the mat; a few inches from a window curtained off by a dark cloth. Sun played in between the warp and woof of the fabric. I almost touched his head, hair dark, lightly curled. While he slept, I worked at what to say. I felt frozen, my 5'9" swelling up and out into one ungainly numbness. (Did this mean I loved him?) Finally I slept.

Matthew was on top of me, so softly, denuding me of my moccasins, my pants and underwear. I pretended to be asleep, because I didn't know what to do, my heart pumping strongly, quietly. Within reach was the word one should say. I would, but my cheeks were hot, my feet cold. I let him slip something in though so quietly, gently, like a wave bringing the mere shadow of itself to the pier piling after its long crashing trip from the sea. He lapped against me—a Zen Epiphany. I held my breath—important not to move forward or back. Just to be, "accept", as he had said, "the moment".

Some tremble of want lit the inside of my thighs that touched his, made me press them in on his to hold him, then died out. I felt stupid for that. We fell asleep.

That afternoon, I followed his lead—dressed and left the bus. He introduced me to his friends inside the Midnight Onion. It was a bar with a stage for folk music at one end. The floors had cinder, people sat at barrel tables. I wove among the tables, jostled one. It had three old beer bottles on it. I wound farther into the long room, semidark even in day. At the end three men again, and a woman. I said so little, they said so little to me, Matthew turned his head and murmured.

He propelled me out of this room, we took a side turn through a kitchen, went outside through a heavy door, and down two concrete steps.

"Here, here's a couple a bucks," he said. "Go out to the

beach. Have fun. Dig in the sand."

He seemed distant. Didn't he like me? I squinted against the bright sun.

"I can work, make a few bucks. We could get some hits. There's a wall beneath the highway. People lay out there. Good people. Get some sun, man." He turned around and left me for the moment.

I walked away. Didn't know if I could get in the bus myself or not, didn't ask. I walked from the Midnight Onion parking lot across the road to the shoulder. A retaining wall dropped off straight down to a wet, dark-sand beach. I looked up and down the road for the way down, saw where the steps were, yards away.

I walked way down the steps; bright and sandy. I couldn't get words out, even inside myself. Everything was so different here. I felt frightened and didn't admit it.

Finally I found a place where it was dry, lay up against the wall, rolled a hole, a trough for myself, and made a sand pillow. Lulled in the sand's chalky heat I thought of how Matthew said, if I took the new psyche-something drug I shouldn't feel frightened. "You might be—like, on a beach, but you might think you were in your parents' home in bed and everything," he'd suggested.

An idea moved up from that leaping, quickening place inside. I still felt the touch of his slight, well-formed shoulder against my back, turned away as he'd been in the bus while we slept.

Would he like me more if I took it with him? I could feel his warmth invade me. I felt good. I dropped to sleep. It was cold dusk when I woke up. I stood. Sand trickled out of my ear. My moccasins had sand in them. I sat against the sea wall and dumped them out. Gulls flapped above me.

Tires, and last winter's debris, clotted the piling beneath the pier to my right and straight out over the sea. I ambled through the sand to the street end of the pier, and walked way, way out on it, over splintered wooden ribs, as though I would walk into the sea. For an instant, I felt sad and old and tired. Some people passed, a teenaged couple and a man with a fishing lure, and one cold-looking child and its mother.

My moccasins padded, the sensation of wood ribs protruding through them. My hands in my pockets, head down I walked and walked, to the end of the pier where there were a few fishermen; I looked down at the slate pate of whirling water.

I wanted to walk farther, like Girl, to embrace the ocean. I shrugged back into the wind. Wind wound strands of hair over my cheek and into my mouth. In anger I spit the sandy strands away. It was darkening when I crossed the road. The Midnight Onion parking lot was filled up. I coughed and stepped up two concrete steps leading to the kitchen, pulling the door open.

"Where you from, little girl?" A man in black turtleneck with a goatee and apron asked in the kitchen.

"From San Francisco," I lied slightly. And no way would I say I was fifteen.

"C'm here." He looked at my length. I had my favorite red and blue stripped velour shirt on over blue jeans, the moccasins and the jacket.

"How old are you?"

"Eighteen."

He smoothed his beard.

"Matthew says you're O.K."

I brightened, tried to smile, my cheeks looked like a little kid's, I thought, like waxy apples. I sucked them in, threw my head back to look gaunt, like the woman with the loom at Esalen.

He turned abruptly toward a big beer keg on the back wall. I slipped through the swing-out door under an arch, into the room at large. Matthew was nowhere around. I propped on a barrel table near the kitchen door, long legs and moccasined feet stretched into the isle.

I felt a pulling from belly out when I thought Matthew's name, like the fear I felt being here. But the pull was from deeper. It scraped up like the razor Matthew had used earlier that day to take away the all-night-beard mask his face had made while we'd driven down the coast with Thor.

Then I felt fear again. It was like being frozen behind a glass. What did they think of me?

The other, pulling feeling took hold. It was a ripple up from between my thighs, a rocking like a mad snake inside hungering to get out. Through these new thoughts and feelings I dissociated somehow, and the fear settled in more comfortably than before.

Matthew came back half past eleven when all the folk shows were finished. I'd sat through four acts, four breaks, only once, after the third, walked up and out toward the musicians, planting each moccasined foot, tough in the cinders.

This group was picking blue grass for the small, tight-packed audience, not jazz. Their back lighting gave an opaque bluish-range effect. When they'd lit cigarettes in between the sets, little orange lights would go off, setting up a interplay of sparks. I could feel the life, the joy, the ease, brush against my face. I slipped closer to the blue-lit men puffing on orange embers, one patting his thigh like a drum.

"Hi," this blond man said.

"Hi," I said shyly.

He smiled. I wanted to go up to him and talk about the music, but disappeared into the recess between kitchen door and table, and sat back down on the keg. I rocked to the last set, legs stretched out straight and long. I sang along and felt, for a moment, happy—maybe this is what I'd come for.

Matthew came and just took my hand and led me back out to the van. There was more pleasure this time, or slipping in and out of him it felt like—like water through the tendrils of seaweed at the bottom of the pier. Just a slipping in and out, through the tendrils of arms and hair, through the breathtaking moment where it slipped through, and would not budge for a moment, then the acquiescing again— then suddenly a great cerebral uproar—trying to be nice while he moved, thinking, "what did he think?" in order to not think, then afterwards sleeping wide awake, feeling like a liar. Later I had a nightmare, and woke, scratching to get out.

Awakened by this just a bit, Matthew regarded me with calm Zen eyes, neither moved to the left, nor to the right, by anything. He stroked my neck for a second and turned away, back into sleep.

At five a.m., after thinking for a long time how uncool I was, unable to get back to sleep after this, afraid to move to the left and wake him, or to the right and wake him, I decided to brush my teeth. I stumbled out of the van towards a faucet at the front of the building.

Cars rumbled in the dark. Water sprayed up from the public water fountain near the curb leading to the beach.

I spread Colgate from a smashed tube onto my brush, bent toward the lush water sparkling in the dark, and then a male voice stormed, "STOP." Heard it out of a hollow in the dark behind me. Hairs erected on my neck. Suddenly the sky was flooded with light. "ORANGE COUNTY SHERIFF," a voice announced.

Chapter 6

"Shall I git her?" asked another.

Hard soles slapped the pavement, then stopped. "No, I'll do it."

On the way to the station I wondered why they hadn't believed me. "What are you doing here?" they'd asked.

"Brushing my teeth. I live here."

"Who owns this place?"

I'd struggled to remember the name of the man with the goatee. "Umm...Nick."

"Nick who?"

"There's no Nick," came a background voice. "We're taking her in as a runaway."

Behind a gray cage in the car separating me from the men, I imagined Matthew's Zen-bland hands behind me, propelling me towards a new vision. I drew in a breath. "Accept," he'd said over and over that night, as we'd wound down the steep bends of cliff highway above deep indigo sea.

"Umm, Matthew, what would you," I'd asked this young master, "if you were like me, living at home with these people who..."

"I'd help my mother when I could. I'd accept." Late morning light had played over his face, a prism dividing the word into a rainbow of possibilities.

Whirring through the still-darkened Orange County streets in the police car, I felt it. "Accept". It was palpable. I tried to apply Matthew's words to the backs of these mute, disgusted-with-me men; I accepted being here, because I was, because it had happened, and the rhythm of the car racing around corners slapped at me, "Accept, Accept, Accept". As they led me to the juvenile hall adjacent to the jail, I stepped out into a wonderful new freedom.

"Bend over," the ladies aid woman ordered me, stripped naked in the shower after the fingerprinting. "Bend over and get it."

"Get what?" I asked, cold in the open shower stall.

"Those bits of soap. You dropped them in the drain. Get them. Get every one."

The woman's voice lingered on the word. I bent sideways, only slightly uncomfortable, still wondering at the wonderful word, "Accept".

"Pick it up." The ice-cold click of keys intruded on my litany. I peeped up through wet hair to the woman's intense stare.

In a twinge of guilt at breaking the rules, I scooped up all the soap shards. I turned the showerhead back on, rinsed my hands, and faced the woman full on.

"May I get out now?"

"Yes...yes. Pick up those clothes you got at the desk." I swept up a stamped pea-green shift with big sleeves, the exact color of my parents' 1960 wagon. I stepped into the underpants, felt dumb-looking, pulled the heavy white bra up in front, clasped it at my navel then swung it around, one hand through a strap at a time. It was dumb, but that was the only way I could do it. The bra felt stiff and made crinkle points under the dress.

"C'm along with me," the woman said, crisp, impatient, like I had asked to spend twenty minutes crouched down, bare, fishing for the soap.

The cell was a room with sunlight through a small barred window lighting a muted orange blanket. I lay, a prisoner of peace and silence, until lunch. Breakfast had been missed within the ritual of soap, dressing and passage through halls toward connecting doors shuddering open after a tight buzz.

I wasn't worried about my parents coming, just digested the new bites of life I'd taken; the blue grass music at the Midnight Onion under blue lights, Matthew's shoulder smooth, white, soft, his hand across my navel, his hand that pulled my blue jeans down, the sounds of the waves slapping entanglements of weed with thick knobby bulbs between the pier pilings. Even the grate separating me in the police car from the men in front, the unsmiling men who twisted my thumb into a smudge of fingerprint loops at the main desk, and again Matthew, his coils of dark hair above Zen-blank eyes that presided somehow much more clearly, than when I was with him, all said, Accept.

With a stub of pencil, I wrote on a piece of toilet paper, it tore. I tried a blank spot on the back of a battered Reader's Digest. "Each moment presents itself to me in peace, I have surrendered to life, or to a step so far beyond me that life has slowed to meet me coming backwards." Other odd wayward thoughts that didn't trouble me at all, flowed across my mind. I heard the sound of a girl calling out, though unclear. It seemed to be from outside. I pressed my face toward the double-grilled window slit, open to the outer yard.

"Who's there?"

"It's me, Tanya," came a voice from the window next door. "Are you the new girl? Can you call my mother in Monterey?"

"I just got here."

"What on?"

"Runaway, I guess."

"Ever been here before?"

"No. I live near San Francisco."

"You'll get out then. My mother won't come. She was here once. I need to call her."

Accept. "You were crying," I said. Can I help you?"

39

"Yeah. Call her. Call my mother. I came here out of a foster home. Shee-it they were mean. Call my mother."

I promised to do so. Took down her number with that stub of pencil on the inside flap of the Reader's Digest. Tanya continued to implore me. "She hasn't been here to see me for six weeks, since they're, they're...talking— a'going, to send me out in a new foster place—"

"I'll call your mom."

Accept.

Everything was a gift. Tanya through the window, the solitude of this room. I lay on the blanket with the empty lunch tray. White bread, bacon, one tomato slice. Not like tea and gruel in the woods at Esalen. But it was good. I ate it. No judgements. I smiled. Jail food was good and Esalen tea and gruel, were good.

I smiled again, like I'd caught the secret everyone wanted to know. Each moment was a gift. I wasn't afraid.

The light through the barred window turned yellow to green. Deep afternoon shadows from the one living tree outside slipped across the concrete yard. I smiled at that too, accepting the floating lights of the dim Orange County sun, though this one great tree they allowed, through this one broad tree splattered by wind, lifted by light and shadow. I accepted the ocean sky deepening as fog washed up from the sea; I watched the white yard cool to blue, and waited for nothing.

After my father's lawyer (Mr. Abogada) came on the plane and got me out, I was even more outcast at home, and though I tried to iron or wash and help out, up against my mother's rage, soon forgot how to accept, and even more identified myself with the outcasts, the fringe, the undesirables in my town.

I met them at St. Michael's Alley, that post-beat dive on University Avenue in Palo Alto where pacifists and poets dropped in and conferred over coffee. The food was often unusual—Greek salads, hamburgers served on those huge purple leaves—always creatively prepared. And the Jukebox played its jazz and select late breaking hits. At home I played Bob Dylan's "Like A Rolling

Stone," over and over again. Here I would put in summer school lunch quarters for Green Onions.

A few dealers hung outside the back door. A French-speaking, very handsome black Haitian and his scraggy red-haired compatriot, sold grass to us few high school kids too. They picked me up from home sometimes—the Haitian and some others—I rode in the back of the van down some frightening streets. I was always afraid of the police with them. Peeking out of the black-draped van—like an enclosed tomb or the Mars Mariner—one night, I could see the lights of MacFarlane's Ice Cream Parlor. We were in downtown Menlo Park, on the magic border, but we'd slipped out; into the watch-out world my mother had so often warned me about.

"Watch out if you go to the park—watch out for old men, they're 'let out' from the Veteran's Hospital. Watch out. Don't you go anywhere near them."

The van slowed. Dark murmuring. A taped-over sandwich bag with what looked like dried summer grass, was pressed into my hand.

"You take this, little girl."

The handsome Haitian's mouldy black eyes stared insouciant laughter at me; his pupils looked like scratched dark brown marbles left in the San Francisquito Creek too long. They'd picked up the dirt of everything. No one could see in.

I'd pass them by, these eyes in this grinning black Peter Paul Belmondo face. But I was a creature of the night, of the little evil that upright white Menlo Park would allow, and I needed these dark compatriots, to slide through the streets with, to fulfill my mother's prophesy that I was "bad" after all—and to see what the night had to offer.

Chapter 7

Berkeley

Months later, after I turned sixteen, I stood in the rain waiting for the uptown bus to Shattuck Avenue. I'd been born near Shattuck Avenue. But the parents who had made me wouldn't want me here—in this new Berkeley where Mario Savio stirred up the Free Speech movement on the Cal campus, where Telegraph Avenue was overrun by a new element, long-haired youths—many not students at all, wearing homemade sandals, Indian pouches and beads, hunching on the sidewalk in front of the Orange Julius stand.

At the bus stop I hugged my new surplus navy pea coat tighter against the rain. I looked the into nimbus the street light made through my contact lenses. Though not on marijuana—grass—or the new stuff I'd been hearing about, I felt high as a power line, soft inside, like the specks of light I saw, floating down from the streetlight through the rain.

I wriggled my feet into snug suede boots with high laces. I

felt swells of excitement and the feeling of racing against something, something just like rain from the streetlight, that racing against being seen, that characterized my life, and the winsome soft delighted feeling, kept me company, kept my fingers strumming words into the pages of the three-ringed, unlined little notebook in my pocket.

I wrote in small letters like e.e. cummings. A graphologist said it was a sign of immaturity. My friend Olive, who'd shown the woman handwriting expert my hand, laughed. "No, not Colly, she's tough."

It was my luck to be seen as tough, or Olive Shreibner—18 and allowed to live away from home by liberal and understanding Jewish parents—would not have let me come to see her almost every weekend.

"I'm going," I would say against my parents' objections. "Only to Olive's house." And I would regale my neurotic mother with some description or other, of Olive's kitchen: the plants, the paintings she'd done at the San Francisco Art Institute, the locks on all the doors. And my mother, who had some respect for art and liberal causes, let me go. Maybe because she needed a respite from the fierce battle of hating me day and night.

I was happy to be let out, to be seeing rainbows around the streetlight, to shudder at the cold coming up in a gust of wind at the Telegraph Avenue stop. The "A" bus would take me to Olive's latest flat–down the hill from activist Jerry Rubin—and this time, maybe, the bus would take me to worlds beyond.

Passing the sorority houses nearer to campus I knew I would never enter one. Unlike the girls at my high school, who were already choosing their college, I doubted I'd get into one, and I wasn't sure I wanted to. I didn't think of college futures or madras plaid skirts and bubble hairdos and who was dating who, like the others at upper crust Atherton High. I was still a teenager. But looks, long, soulful looks would pour out of me. As I looked out the bus window into the eyes of an old bum, his gray-encrusted coat moulding about his wet feet, or at a Chinese woman with crackling dot eyes and a shopping bag full of hardened loaves, I wanted to write.

And I would write poetry on the bus, stringing the images

of these people together—these two lost people, in my songs, jewels strung between nothing but the wisdom, the purity, the beauty that poured out of their eyes to me. No plot, I guess, no point, but I liked to lift them onto my page like the fried eggs at the diner at the "A" stop, lift them onto hot bread, scoop them up and swallow them up into me. Making poems about the people I saw out the bus window, was like lining empty dark reaches inside, like creating a secret cache with verbal threads like in the tapestry bags the vendors sold on Telegraph Avenue. The poems' bright, soulful designs would keep me busy the next week back in high school. We rumbled to a wheezing stop at Telegraph Avenue.

I met Olive across from the classic movie theatre. She walked slowly, shorter than I, dark, almost black wavy hair a curtain that separated her solemn face at its part. "I'd like to look like you," Olive had said when we first met at the Pacific progressive school my parents let me attend those brief six months.

Like to look like me—I'd thought she was making fun of me. My mother had braided my thoughts with my inadequacies; by fifteen I'd thought I was ugly. Walking up Telegraph Avenue, I glanced in store windows and saw myself and Olive standing free from the knots of people walking just before and just behind us.

I was nearly 5'9" by now, my hair long down the back of my pea coat changing back to all light brown from when I'd dyed it black when I'd tried to be a greaser. My back was straight, my legs were long, I should have thought I was pretty. Olive looked at me with dark, glimmering, sparkly eyes. She thought so. Maybe that's why she wanted me to be her friend.

The high school reject inside me never followed more than a foot behind. As we walked, I found myself thinking unkind things about Olive too: she didn't feel pretty, no one wanted her either—things like that—I took great satisfaction in cracking my boot heels. Click, clack, I felt tough, tall, Colly against them all.

No one wants her wasn't exactly true, I thought later when we leaned that night against the wall, lounging on her single mattress on the floor in her Berkeley apartment—how cool. She recounted the long list—it had gotten longer—of the guys she'd had sex with. Then I took out mine—mostly mental—and I too, added on. We giggled, analyzed ourselves for counting at all, and said goodnight.

I slept in an extra sleeping bag and pillow she'd put on the floor beside her bed. I felt as safe in that drafty apartment with too many glass windows that would let the early morning sun in, as I usually did with anybody—probably more.

That morning sun streamed down upon us and woke us too soon, warmed our toes to hot. We were late sleepers in those days. How wonderful the first time I'd slept over at her cultured Jewish parents' home on the mid-peninsula. Her mother had greeted us at almost twelve, with none of the guilt my mother dished.

"You two have had a lovely sleep." Years later, in the therapy group her mother led, and I'd attend, this kind Jewish mother would say to me when I "worked on" the agony of being abruptly awakened by my mother—a Sominex and wine crazed Joan Crawford-like banshee—"You poor, poor child, sleep is sacred."

Maybe I came to Olive's these weekends, just to sleep, just to be away from the screaming, the gnawing, wearing-down fights, the fear, the lack of safety in the house in Tupper's Park on Darkwood Lane. This summer I was going to Mexico, had talked my parents into being an exchange student. But this was the only refuge I had till then. At Olive's I always got back some sleep, some of myself, some spirit of home, when there was no home, I was offered some shelter, from an eighteen-year-old girl in some ways as woeful as myself. It was more parallel play at being grown up, a branching of parallel fantasies, that led us here together.

An hour later Olive made tea in the bright early morning kitchen light. I turned my face to the side, always aware— my mother had taught me—bright light made me look ugly. "A young girl's face should look fresh and smooth," she had complained, peering through the rear view mirror when driving my sister and me away from the tract where we lived when I was twelve.

"Look at your face," my mother had derided, pointing to my bumpy cheeks, contorted with anger, shame and confusion.

My face was more or less bumpless now, but I avoided bright lights, because I could still feel imagined, crater-like imperfections. "Do you want an egg?" Olive asked. An egg. Sure. I drummed my fingers on the wooden table slab set up on supports. Olive's father had the table sent up to Berkeley for her. Olive was a carpenter; she'd gotten to live at home behind her parents' house in a cabin she and her dad had built by hand. That little cabin in her parent's yard had been to us, a pad. A warm and mellow place where we could hang out, home in the afternoon and evenings after Pacific High that rolled across low hills beneath the Skyline Boulevard fogline above Woodside.

The school owners had gotten us kids building things. Olive was handy at everything practical about which I knew nothing—carpentry, growing squash, stretching canvas and cooking.

"Umm," Olive looked up at me over our eggs, out of the tent made by her voluminous dark hair. "I'm going to the Vietnam Day Committee House on Ashford Street. Do you want to come?"

"Yeah, OK. What do you do there, Olive?"

"I'm making anti-war posters. There's going to be a peace march next Friday. They need a few more posters." Olive was an artist.

"Will they care if I come?"

"They may need you too, Colly."

After breakfast, Olive and I left her porch apartment, down three steps outside, through a walkway surrounded by low hedges. We walked up the three blocks swelling higher toward Channing Street and the Vietnam Day Headquarters. Rather I strode.

Olive walked briskly to keep up with me, her hands pushed down in her puffy gray jacket—a gift from her mother for warmth. Olive pulled a sliced apple in waxed paper out of her pocket—her habit to clean her teeth, even after the braces. She offered me some. I declined. She chewed it deliberately. We trudged upward past a sorority house.

A sorority girl cut in front of our path going toward the sorority steps. Perfectly coifed, she wore white lipstick, curled eyelashes, and a Peter Pan collar shirt— madras plaid over a culotte skirt a half inch above the knees. That's what "Seventeen Magazine" was showing.

Olive and I looked at each other and masked chuckles. "Maxine Factor," I quipped. Olive's eyes sparkled over her apple slice. "Ra-ra Revlon."

This was the life we disdained. The girl stepped into the pristine house in a flash of white socks and polished penny loafers.

"She probably had pennies in them too, Olive, shiny pennies, with the date of her sweet sixteen birthday party on one, and her debutante ball date on the other."

"Yeah," Olive added—we loved to make up stories—"her first ball was in Hillsborough."

"But her first ball—if at all, will be here."

Olive chortled at the Miller-like sex talk we'd been learning and spit out apple seeds all over the unblemished sidewalk in front of the Sigma Sigma Pi House.

I kept up my jabs at the sorority girl, all the way to the steps of Jerry Rubin's Vietnam Day Committee House. Then, like I'd reached a national shrine, I stopped to tie my dangling bootlaces.

This is the most wonderful day of my life, I suddenly thought. An unkempt profusion of yesterday's flowers spilled out over the concrete box that formed a wall above the sidewalk and along the steps up to the dilapidated two-story building.

I followed Olive who walked up each step with a deliberate lift of her foot, like a small boy soldier. Her lacy brass earrings glittered beneath her ears, sparkled within shiny black and indigo hair.

A bearded man sprawled across a foyer opening into a living room scattered with newspapers, ashes, ashtrays. The walls were plastered with posters. "Who's this?" the bearded guy asked.

"This is Colly—she's cool."

I wanted to laugh, but Olive had gotten me in. On a wall near the front bay window was a huge collage. I came near and stared. There was President L.B.J., his nose a warship missile, amid napalmed babies. The ugliness of him radiated out like stinging chemicals, his eyes like twin germs, polluted everything he touched. That was the man my parents watched on the news, a man who dressed in the same suits as my dad.

In that dirty room I was afraid for an instant—whom to trust? In another instant, I transferred the fear to the poster, and knew its creators were right. This caricature president looked mad, and happy about it, like he'd drunk children's blood.

The filthy bilge bloating his face was made up of minute Vietnamese corpses or their amputated limbs, and by pen lines enumerating his crimes and defining his face.

No one had ever called out a president before. No one I'd ever known. I looked out onto the street, wondered in which cars, or behind which hedges, the police were hiding.

Olive chewed another apple slice, the same stolid way she'd built her back yard cabin. That reassured me, but my eyes were churning, tears of anger welled up behind them. Why hadn't they told me how bad our government was?

"We need sixty more posters, girls. Can you make them?" The listless man from the foyer had moved. He lounged against a wall, long legs stretched out toward a worn, dust-colored sofa. He barely looked up for a reply. "The markers are in the back."

We filed through a room with two women in it, three desks, two manual typewriters and more stacks of papers and books than I had ever seen. At the far back was a kitchen, with steps downward into an enclosed porch.

"That's Steve," Olive was quieter than usual after we left our host. "They're all tired. They've been up for days getting ready for the march."

Chapter 8

Berkeley, 1966

Anti-Vietnam Day Rally at last. A littered marketplace on a Saturday afternoon. I skipped down Telegraph Avenue—at 3:00 for the big anti-Vietnam demonstration. Dr. Benjamin Spock, author of the liberal baby manuals that changed childrearing in our generation, would speak.

Throngs wound in and out of the Orange Julius shop, pressed six deep to the counter for a chance to eat, and were released back onto the sidewalk, some with hot dogs and orange froth, some with nothing. A few lucky kids ate at tables but most just crouched close to the counter for a moment, dug into bowls of crisp onions and mustard, shlepped them onto their hotdogs and ran out.

At the entrance to Telegraph after we crossed at the light, carts of delicacies brought hope to the still hungry. We waved our hand across somebody shorter, handed someone a dollar, got a quarter back, got a good falafel—what's that?—It must be food, though—and ate it, loping across the avenue toward the open field that held Dr. Ben Spock aloft on a rickety platform, while Malvina Reynolds sang a folk song or two. "Little boxes made of ticky tacky." Like our parents' houses in suburbia.

Overcast closed against the brightness. Long-haired women looked so sleek, serious and sure, at sixteen I admired their serenity, stared into their faces to catch some of it, like light.

A wisp of cloud wound around our group in a big cirrus circle, like God—marking the spot. Brightness streamed in from a tiny hole above, over the podium and into the first few rows.

Spock talked to us. Tall, graying, he was a nice man, like our fathers. He'd written the baby books we'd been raised on, now he addressed us—his results. But he was for us, too. The warmth, like a little rainbow in the bright glow between the surrounding clouds, played over his sparkling, silvering hair.

Our young faces in the deep coagulation of bodies from there back, were serious and still, washed in gray. We waited like a whole body for its head. For wisdom to reach each cell with a thought, true thought. We'd all crowded here, drawn by word of mouth, many of us not understanding the pull that had made us come. Until Spock spoke and a marching rhythm coursed through our collective consciousness.

After Spock spoke, I was ready to march. I looked down at my newly sandaled feet and felt sure of them. We precocious children who'd come into the world after the shock of World War II, had at last found a father we could respect, look up to. We were hungry for the few people older than ourselves who hadn't bought the post war materialism of our parents. We found them here in inspiring figures like Malvina Reynolds and Benjamin Spock; they were forerunners, bright, spots of singular light. They looked out on their soul children and claimed us.

This adoption brought a surge of filial feeling. Over the next year we would find courage to do the unexpected—create more radical rallies at what would become People's Park, get maced. Some U. C. Berkeley students would follow Mario Savio, sacrifice study time, demonstrate at Sproul Hall. Others would be regulars at the Anti Vietnam Day Committee, some of us would be clubbed outside the Oakland Induction Center.

I did not belong in the age group of that movement. Compared to them, I was just a little kid waiting for her luck to turn, looking for parents I could trust. My personal deprivation and my soul and civic responsibilities fit right together. But with the rest that night, I was ready to march.

The First Anti-Vietnam March: a swirling human spiral swept the streets with new hope. At the rally the folksingers had sung about how, from the beginning of time, warmongers each believed they had God on their side. They'd sung about Germans and Russians, and ourselves, each hating the other, pointed out the irony of each one being right, gently denounced the concept of war. Today, pushed ahead by the others in the front row, I knew we were right. This night, we had God on our side.

By the next day I was convinced we had changed the entire world. I was dismayed when the San Francisco Chronicle said there were only 3,000 of us. We knew there had been 10,000 or more. But by now we were learning the Establishment lied.

Afterward Olive took us to Jerry Rubin's place in the hills. It was all a blur except talking to Karl in front of Rubin's fridge. I'd met the 22-year old graduate teaching assistant on the March. Karl was barely medium height, dark, curly-haired and good looking. His mother had been in a Nazi camp in Belgium. He already taught psychology, had a dream his anima was calling to him over his mother's fears.

On New Year's Eve, I came back to his careful studio apartment. He tried gentle, protected sex with me that night and a few times afterwards. I admired him, but he really wanted an actual woman. Even though I listened to the Beatles' Dylanesque introspective, "Norwegian Wood" repeatedly–"I once had a girl, or should I say, she once had me," I was too young.

I told Mak from Tupper's Park about him. Mak became jealous, invited me to North Beach, to City Lights bookstore again, said we'd stop for coffee at a friend's apartment. To punish my independence, he date raped me.

"Stop it."

"If I pull out you won't get pregnant."

With a missed period and nowhere to turn, I called the young professor Karl who helped me secure a very early abortion. In a daze weeks after the abortion, I agreed to meet him on Graduation Day at the U.C. campus. He'd heard about Leary's experiments at Harvard, wanted to try a psychedelic drug. And that guy ahead of me at Pacific High School—Bob Weir—played with his new band, The Grateful Dead, at some kind of "test" at the Fillmore Auditorium in San Francisco, everybody talked about it.

I'd danced strobe at the Rock For Peace there benefiting Democratic candidates and Vietnam peace groups. Quicksilver Messenger Service, Big Brother and the Holding Company had pulsed out at us.

Since I'd met Karl on the March, I'd learned more about his mother, about his belief men were streamlined, we both agreed I was lucky to be with a man, when he had to deal with a female for love, it was messier than dealing with a male mind, women were like his mother. I idolized him.

But despite coming tentatively with a man for the first time on New Year's Eve—if it didn't work I was going to give it up forever—he wanted a woman his age who lived on a houseboat in Sausalito.

I wanted to see him again, and assured him over his doubts, that I was ready to take it too.

In the new daylight, 16 years old, I cried on Karl's bed, my face buried in a towel. I cried like from the belly pouring up the throat. Is this what the Drug can do, I thought? But then the thought was gone in an odd way, leaving a faint memory that something had been there, only, and I cried again.

He was still patient, dark, 22, Jewish, assistant professor, but everything had changed. He sat with me on the bed and exchanged one towel for another when it became that wet.

"Maybe that's good for you, to cry," he offered, then looked at his watch. "Time to go. I've got to get you to your train. Please tell me where your things are."

I couldn't remember. I'd taken a dose of the Drug with him on graduation day on the U.C. Berkeley campus twenty hours before, and now I cried as though the cry had been held in for centuries.

He drove me to the train station. "Will I see you again, in September?" I pleaded. He said nothing to me, just smiled kindly.

I wasn't aware of riding the train at all, then my father picked me up and came into focus, listening to a country music station real, real soft. I thought the hallucinations were over, but when he looked at me, hate burned out of one eye and turned it bright red. Oh, he's crazy, I thought, I knew my mother had driven him to this, and I knew he hated what I was doing. To block out the guilt I made myself think he was L.B.J. with the missile on his nose, and I hated him too.

At the house I lost all sense of time. Before the drug, the days couldn't have passed too quickly until the trip to Mexico. But now I was only aware of fragments of time.

I remember being at the swimming pool with Mak whom my mother hated, though she didn't know he'd made me pregnant. He spent all his days on grass now, had used that as an excuse to lose the pregnancy urine test. His family was Catholic anyway, he would have wanted a child, but I couldn't think about that now.

I saw the long shadows on the grass in the park where we had been young together with our families hating us. Today I saw the lines of the shadows sickeningly elongate farther and farther than I knew they could, or should.

"Makky, I'm frightened," I whispered, couldn't say more.

"It's all right," he said with new tenderness. He usually told me my faults—I guessed because he hated himself so much—his father hating him—and I was the nearest thing to a friend he had.

"I couldn't marry anyone who hadn't taken it," he whispered, and I smiled back at him, aware of the tragedy we both shared now.

My mother, could I call her that, must have sensed something. Once I came to, sitting up straight in the bed in the morning, long after I should have left. "What's the matter with you?" she screeched. "Don't you ever fool around with drugs now, or you'll be a mindless vegetable. Do you hear me? A vegetable."

Oh God. Why do I say God? Is there God? Could he hear Me? God, if you're there, hear me.

Three days later I left for Mexico on a plane and when the plane took off it seemed to me like the Drug, but a man latched onto me; men always did and the man and I talked. I guess I sounded like what people told me I was. "Awfully precocious." We talked about the ruin at Xochimilco. He invited me by if I got out that way.

By the time I arrived I'd almost forgotten the horrible cargo I had with me, but the "flashing" started after I got settled in a room in Mexico City with the family that had agreed to take me in for school. I only saw the daughter, but became aware through a few words exchanged in the skinny little courtyard, that I was to pay them, leave them alone. Just as well.

I was on my way over to the drugstore across the busy, inner city street, off to read something, maybe an English magazine, when it began. My consciousness lifted off like a nightmare airplane. I took myself back, to the rooftop somehow and crouched there like a child, half in fetal position, trying not to fall off. My sense of balance itself, was precariously tipped, and I could not see where the edge was, inside or out.

SAN FRANCISCO
BERKELEY
MENLO PARK / PALO ALTO
MONTEREY
BIG SUR

UNITED STATES OF AMERICA

VENICE
ORANGE COUNTY

MEXICO

PUERTO VALLARTA
MEXICO CITY
MANZANILLO

ACAPULCO

Chapter 9

Not in my right mind, just surviving, an hour later I moved down the stairwell and rushed across the city street into a drugstore. Mario Hector Gongoro Gonzales introduced himself at the counter. He was a 22-year-old intern at Central Surjurico and had some English, my Spanish was better. In the next two weeks I learned Spanish for life. He moved me from the family across from the drugstore into a flat owned by an Aleman—or German woman, whom I came to suspect as an ex-Nazi.

He called me "Mami," took me to operations, an abortion ironically, and a hip replacement. In the operating room he caught me when I fainted at the first sight of the saw. He crept into the German boarding house, wrecking my reputation, and he took me to the West Coast on holiday, renting a hotel and asking me over and over, "Does you daddy drive a car with fins?"

He helped me enroll in the University of Mexico, at the hub of a city covered with Diego Rivera's huge murals. One Mexican history class was taught by a full-bodied woman in a tight dress with rich leg hair coiled under her stockings. In another class on Pablo Neruda I met new friends—Ariel Zuniga, grandson of a great revolutionary, son of a great sculptor, and two American youths, a Jewish girl from the east and a Nordic looking boy from the west. I didn't want to hear about the car with fins anymore and embraced these new friends, drifting away from Mario and the hospital.

Without Mario's protection the Nazi woman threw me out for talking to her young Indian maid about better wages. With nowhere to go, I holed up with other Americans from the University in a cheap high-rise apartment.

A plain, serious, full-faced male student from a mid-western Bible College was on the lease, a friend of his with manic-depressive disorder stayed over, and the rest of us flowed in and out.

The Bible guy took me with him to the outskirts of town to meet an old Indian woman who sold psychedelic mushrooms. He'd never had a sexual experience before, and after our night together he remained a virgin. He was nice, but he wasn't cool, and his nervousness and repression held sway.

After that, I hung around with the seventeen-year-old Jewish girl and the nineteen-year-old guy from California. One night, after Debra went back to her uncle's hotel, Nors and I came back to the high rise to crash. The neurotic student had stopped taking his lithium and regaled us with a bizarre kitchen sculpture he'd made from spoons, to represent chess and his girl friend.

Only thing was, he added paper and cardboard to it in the night and lit it afire. We had to force the heavy metal hall door open for the leaky Mexico City fire hoses.

Coming back to get our things, Nors and I saw the kid let out from the mental hospital the next day. Banging against the buildings, his sweat and paint streaked face was a blur of psychotic, tranquilized hyper euphoria. With nowhere to go and a break from school, Nors and I took to the road.

The first night out, Nors pushed me down onto a bed in a deep dark room. High clay ceiling, sheets of uncertain cleanliness. Nors stripped out of the white sailor skivvies he always wore.

Each button opened up more of a silky amber–colored thicket of hair. I was cool—I'd look. If those writer guys could do it, I'd do it, and use tough names too. I wrote in my head, "A long golden prick hung from a wide flesh base among the curls."

He approached me, gripping the thing, rolling it in the almost dark between his palms. As a child I'd rolled out a snake of play dough on a rainy day. There was tropical rain outside. Nors' blond Dutch boy hair shadowed Julie Christie lips. He braced his legs wide and regarded me.

How'd I get here? I wanted to ask, but stripped instead under the unfamiliar sheet and army issue blanket.

He rolled the thing, like an unpeeled plantain whose smooth golden skin hid iridescent, sensitive fruit. The head peeked out, swollen, from between the receding foreskin folds, crowning, like a birthing infant.

Startled at the analogy, I turned away. Nors thought of himself as the new Dean Moriarty—after his hero of the beat book, On The Road. Nors' manly display, somehow infantile? At this thought—not the frontal display—I felt myself blush.

He sprang into bed, long knees tent poles that lifted the sheets. He made tunnels for his long hands. His fingers wriggled into my orifices. Trying to be cool and not tense up and just go along with it, it became a story in my head.

He peeled the skin back, I heard the words, he slid the moist golden-blond plantain tip into me, rode it into a little bramble of light brown hair that covered a pink flesh cave, its promontories and wet ridges licking and inflaming the exposed tongue. I'd read that stuff, the male view like that, poetic sometimes but always the male view.

Nors mounted deeper into me, slid it, oblivious to me, in a heightened rhythm. He pressed, a thoughtful lost child in his dark-muted orgasm, smiled, through the Julie Christie lips, proffered, "You're not bad."

His mood was mine. I sensed that Debora, the seventeen–year old Jewish student he'd hoped would come on the road with us, was forgotten for the moment, and even his lost love, that

61

other "clitoral Jewess who left me to become a Lesbian", had paled somewhat, in his thoughts.

"Move over", he nudged, slapped a long arm across my buttocks and entered a dreamlike state; I imagined the foreskin of his conscious awareness peeled back, to penetrate the intuitive mysteries of the night.

Hitchhiking the next day, we waited awhile at the side of the jungle road. A Mexican man and his son picked us up. We sped down the ribbon of road over jungle hills toward Acapulco. The son drove. His gold-toothed father egged him on.

The car careened down the faded dividing line in the road like a Cape Kennedy missile gone mad. At the crest of the hills before the absolute drop through great jungle to the sea, the father screamed to his son in Spanish, "Rolando, brake the car."

The men hopped out. Rolando y Rolando—the son had the father's name—ran to a low hut with corrugated metal roof set in a rare clearing in this foliage.

"Ola Ernesto!"

In response, a dumpy man in soiled white, lumbered out of the house. The two older men exchanged a few words and ran to an unsuspecting cow grazing on the ocean side of the cleared hill. Rolando Sr. squatted, fat rolls lumping up his pants. "Ernesto, Ernesto—ayuda me."

Ernesto hauled out an unglazed crock and our chauffeur refueled himself with amber-looking milk. The cow looked annoyed.

Nors sauntered up, three heads taller than the rest. He took the crock, threw his golden head back and downed the whole uncertain mess, swinging backwards, legs straddled as if on deck.

Nors always steadied himself with powerful gestures molded from an interrupted stint in the Navy. In a moment they were back in the car. The door clanged shut. Crowded against Nors, I smelled manure de vacas and warm milk.

Better than the odor that emanated from Rolando Sr. and his son, whom he still flailed with his voice, to take the turns at increasing speeds.

I wondered if they'd ever had a car before, or if this was even their car, the way they abused it, and my nerves on the sharp turns. These Mexicans were all jazzed up by cars and modern possessions, the way North Americans had been decades before. Their car could have been the first television set in Tupper's Park, everyone all lined up in the Crocker's living room in 1953 to extract as many laughs from Lucy as was humanly possible, or swoon in childish glee as Gleason was sucked right there, into the room after the theme song from The Honeymooners.

When Nors and I were finally dumped off on a street corner in downtown Alcapulco by the macho Rolandos, I could have rolled into Nors' navy seabag and been carried. I'd had it.

Instead, we sat, at Nors' suggestion—under the influence of On The Road—on a street corner, in the heart of the downtown, crouching over the high curb.

"Let's see what's goin' on, let's see what's goin' on," Nors intoned.

In the late afternoon we sipped tall cups of agua de aroz hailed from the vendor who circled this intersection. Cool, white-sandaled feminine feet, jauraches, Texan boots and topsiders slid by in slow motion. The delicious agua had cooled me. I looked about.

Lights flickered on. The street assumed a carnival air. A hippie couple suddenly sat beside us on my side of the curb.

"I'm McGee," a long, lanky, tousled boy, narrower than Nors, suggested in a sleepy voice.

"And I'm Curlie."

They were hustlers, who begged here regularly. Friendly, they quickly told us—rather, me—everything about themselves. Nors was buried in existential cool. Glad just to be here at last, he was neither looking forward nor backward in time, just digging this new scenery. He was "on the road".

ACAPULCO '66

Curlie and McGee had met in a mental hospital in Vermont.
Somehow they'd gotten out, "fucked" in the woods. "Bobby didn't
have to be taught," Curlie purred, "he knew how — just from hisself."
How Curlie came to talk like she heralded from North Carolina, I
did not know, but so did many Californian suburban hippies too,
so no matter.

Curlie, tiny, frizzy-haired, small-breasted doll in a gingham
dress and bare feet, ran her crooked finger up McGee's vertebrae.
He smiled. In my same new way like the guy writers way, I could
see him, happy at last, wedging his whole thing in, banging at

64

Curlie's little smooth "snatch" upturned to him like a jelly roll. The hip male authors I'd barely read were fast becoming the language of my imagination.

When they had dragged them back to the mental hospital, it must have been in a sex stupor, because it took them three more weeks to get out this last time. McGee set it up. He'd had a taste, nothing could keep him from her. From her cunt, that's how they'd say it, Miller and the like.

The night of the breakout, they'd run through the woods of Vermont to freedom. Curlie had been stripped half-naked on the barbed wire on the edge of the hospital grounds, ran clutching together the shards of her court-issue shift. But they'd made it, and were here, begging, and presumably, fucking.

Later I realized they were not above hustling sexual favors. That's what had gotten her into the mental hospital in the first place—making it with the well-to-do locals in the town for pocket change. Stirred up a bit but frustrated by youth and numbness and Nors, and wanting to say it in hard sexual terms, I couldn't look at them after and not feel the entanglement—that long boy McGee, and Curlie's smug little all-weather snatch he'd just filled. I was seeing myself and other females the way these literary guys did. But I was also in a hard-edged world.

So I thought, they radiated their balling. When they kissed, they sucked audibly like a snug coitus and he fondled her little long-nippled tits through her Sunday-school dress while she slithered slight hips and rubbed up on him. These advertisements no doubt made hustling their obvious profession in the tourist-clotted streets of sixties Acapulco.

Stimulated by the excursion to Acupulco, after the last University of Mexico class, we were on the road for real. This time to Puerto Vallarta, where The Night of the Iguana had been filmed. From Guadalahara west by prop plane.

But we left Puerto Vallarta in a few days. Although the beach was strewn with umbrellaed drink stands, huge shells and lapped by warm ocean, the extremes of rich and poor had turned us off. One night some European jet-set kids had taken us to a pricey villa on the hilltop, the next day we watched gold toothed Mexican youths pelting a poor dwarf man with rotten vegetables. We'd come in by plane, left by jungle bus. As with our hitchhiking experience with the Rolandos, the bus driver stopped in a mountain ravine and he and all the Mexican passengers disappeared into the jungle for hours at siesta time, leaving us with the chickens.

After the jungle bus, we hitched. By nightfall, Nors and I hopped off the flat back of a long, '40's-style truck into this, the tiniest village. Its lights were darkened.

At a street corner, we stopped outside a small hut with one neon sign. Nors peered into the dark cafe. "Where is the hotel, place to sleep?" he called in Spanish. The apron-clad owner came out, pointed across the street to what appeared to be a vacant lot with something low huddled into the night under 10,000 stars.

We ran across the unpaved street, leaped. I felt good, swept high by the tiny pinpricks of light, unfamiliar with the palpable sound of village sleep and heavy desolation.

We stepped over collapsed adobe brick that formed a low–walled opening to the night sky courtyard. At the far end, an old woman slapped tortillas by candlelight.

"This is your hotel. We sleep here," Nors spoke to me in Spanish with an Indian accent. Already he was one of them. I didn't feel like one of them at all, just wonderfully alone.

With a fierce, stubborn visage, the woman asked for a tiny amount of money—like we wouldn't give it. We handed her what she asked for—80 cents American. She pointed, murmured instructions, and we walked diagonally to the farthest, darkest corner of the yard.

As I drew nearer, I saw the wall was not a wall at all, but was interspersed with several doors, closely spaced. It was so dark that I did not see how Nors opened our door, but passed inside and was coated with a dusty velvet darkness. He closed the door behind us.

It was as solemn as a shrine. Nors struggled with one of two remaining matches in his book. One sputtered, the other showed us a candle on a round pottery base. He lit it, and we looked about in the dimness.

There was a raised ledge like a board for sleeping, and it was covered with one very old blanket. Nors put our bag between the wall and us, extinguished the light, took his navy issue blanket from his bag and we slowly–clothes on–sandwiched in between the two bedcoverings.

Next door to our hollow, closed room, a man moaned and paced, moaned and paced. "O, Santa Maria, Santa Maria, Madre de Dios"—and the rest was inaudible, muffled by pain sounds and tears. At three a.m., Nors slipped out. He returned, felt sweaty and shaky to touch.

"I saw the man next door," he whispered. "There was blood on his side–he was clutching his shirt. We sleep poised for action until first light."

We left early to escape the moaning. In the new light we found we were not far from Manzanillo. We trudged our stuff away from the stone wall motel, away from the tiny cafe with its ghostly Coca Cola sign in the middle of nowhere to turn down a road where we waited again, to be borne farther–and further–on our journey.

Chapter 10

Mexico, 1966

We watched the black prow of the Greek ship cut through the blue-green and amber waters of Manzanillo Bay. We stood on the roped-off cement walkway at the edge of the wooden dock and smiled up in awe. The gray bow stopped three stories above us.

At night the hanging lights of the town reflected in the water, danced blue and orange and white in our eyes. Stars pinpointed the black sky. A fresh warm salty breeze blew through the docks from the sea, swept back into the Town Square where mariaches thumped and innocent young girls walked in twos around a lantern-lit promenade.

Next morning a gull flew overhead. Water lapped at the pilings beneath our feet. I wriggled my toes in the new rubber tire juaraches Nors had bought for me the day before.

In 1966, Manzanillo was little more than a fishing village, even though it was a channel for train cars of goods fed to the town from inland ranches toward the Greek and Japanese and Scandinavian ships. Sometimes the Scandinavian sailors gave the town a curly yellow-haired mesclada child or two, before they left. Other than these children, the town had few if any rubelitas, or fair-haired people, and certainly few Norteamericanos. The people stared at Nors and me, but with no notion to connect us to, left us alone.

Our room was above the train yard that fed the ships. It was in the top floor of one of the old buildings. The plain room that twisted into an open door shower stall at the end across from the windows, contained only a bed and a rickety bureau. We found flowers to fill the bowl someone had left. The splintering dutch windows opened out over the noises of the tracks, looked out over a great expanse of sea. The ocean alternately churned lacy white froth or swelled into irregular see-through tubes or ridges, like the ones left in our blanket after we were done making love.

I guess you could call it that. I was too young to know the rights of my own body and Nors foiled my sweaty attempts to guide his body to mine. At eighteen, two years older, he spoke to me from the position of superior knowledge. Having served in the Navy, he said if you liked "that," you should go be a lesbian.

I backed away and settled for warmth and dim fulfillment. Sweat poured off us in the bed, onto the floor when we stood, commingled with the sweet cold water from the showerhead when we bathed. Still, I slept next to Nors because I was far from home and the slickness of his indifferent body in sleep offered a slight anchor against my fears.

Half-asleep I felt that we would slip out over the sea and fall in, or, because of the strange upward slant of the room towards the window, that the ink blue swollen sea would slide into the room, gallon by gallon, and smother us like the sweat-drenched blue blanket we lay under.

But something from beneath the window, from the sky made only of heavy waters as viewed from the bed, had drawn me from the relative wealth of my parents' home in California, had driven me to be stronger than my brother and sister who nightly witnessed ugliness and rage from our battling parents—far more twisted than any of the dwarfs or legless beggars who shocked me here, running on squat legs, rolling on wooden planks through the Mexican streets. Something, raw joy, filled me; under the old blue blanket I listened late at night to the quay whisper and list. Two nights after we arrived, I stood with Nors beneath the prow of the ship, heard the lap of white water against the pilings, looked beyond the lights of the town festival at the stars, saw them sprinkle a visual cacophony of newborn, vibrant color, like salt, into the living waters of the bay. The lights seemed to quiver, splay and whorl, to signal change for Nors and me—for the young people of our own country, for mankind.

Nors grabbed my hand with unusual warmth. "Tomorrow we'll go aboard and see what she's brought in," he said, radiant.

We turned and walked up the shadowed cut of street by the tracks beneath the overhanging hillside. I shivered. I would have to hold tight to Nors tonight under his sea blanket. I knew I wouldn't sweat, not even in the tropical August heat. The shiver was too deep.

This shiver had something to do with the Greek freighter; it shifted on the same swells that had already threatened to drag me from my window. Now the sea had an agent, the tall, gray-prowed ship. I shook for a moment as we entered the alleyway leading to the crooked steps up to our poor hotel room.

I reached for Nors' hand but it was attached to a voice that was singing a far-away sea song of his Norwegian ancestors. Morning was white blue, and shimmered in waves. Brown skinned children played, skipped over the railroad tracks. They seemed made for the heat, like beats of regular rhythm within the waves of shimmering sound only skin could hear.

The Manzanillans must have thought, if they thought anything at all, that Nors was an enormous albino, turned red like a crab's belly by every breath of cool, new morning sun. Some Indian people had a way of simulating no thought, could appear blanker than the sea, which changes, more stubborn and unrelenting than tropical insects, when they stared into the face of someone strange. If they hadn't seen anyone like you before, it was better. And they simply didn't see us at all. We had to go on doing what we were doing, with no opportunity to project self-doubt onto the disapproving faces of those we saw.

Nors and I were invisible in Manzanillo that summer. Ignored by the Mexicans, we were welcomed by other foreigners.

"Efharisto," the captain yelled—good morning, good day, in Greek—and invited us to come on board. We had bathing suits under our clothes because the days had grown so humid that we had to walk in suits by noon. Nors asked if we could swim. "Yah," was all the black and gray-haired man said.

We leaped from a great height into the relieving water. We paddled in the close space between the Greek and another, Japanese freighter. The captain and some younger men clapped. We floated in the brine to show off, after the first dive, after we found there were rungs laid into the ship's side and we could climb back up.

We stretched out on towels. Nors read his floppy copy of Jack Kerouak's On The Road. I slept.

I jerked, dreamed that the giant ship rolled over us as we swam. In the dream, I flailed in a cloudy green-blue water, trying to catch onto Nors, whose feet dangled way above me. His book drifted down to me.

I wrapped around it like a fetus, sank down through the wan, fish-filled water to the bottom. I panicked. My eyes popped open.

Nors was still reading. Unfamiliar blue sky pressed down on me. I thought I'd go inside so I wouldn't burn.

I found the captain sitting in his mess, where he had allowed us to eat lunch with him earlier. Nors had said, that was a great honor. The captain sat at a small table bracketed to the deck, and read. I thought that odd. The book didn't seem to be a merchandise manual but rather a small volume of something that looked like poetry. He smiled at me, formally. I said nothing, couldn't.

"You go to Japan, with me." He smiled, gleaming white teeth. "Nors too, maybe?" He smiled again. Double leathery creases framed his mouth.

I shivered, harder than last night in the alley. "Yasso—" which meant thank you, I replied. Then, "No, no, no." I shook my head. But I smiled, remembering to appear cool. No! I remembered the dream, felt myself slowly sinking, wrapped around Jack Kerouak's book, slowly, slowly panicking. "My mother. My father. I have to get home," I said. He thanked me for the meal we'd had earlier. That was odd. I smiled again, pressed his outstretched hand and fled back to the leeward deck to find Nors.

"Nors, Nors, come here." The captain hadn't followed me out, I could see.

Nors emerged.

"He wants us to go with him!" I sounded alarmed. Nors beamed.

"Go with them!" His eyes looked far away, past the docked Japanese ship to the real Japan.

"Nors!"

"You'd never have to see your old lady again." Nors smiled out of his thick Julie Christie lips. His wan eyes looked thoughtful, though opaque. I never could see through his eyes.

"Nors, come on. Even I want to go back. Maybe not to her, but I have friends, man." I could tell he was pleased by my cool, and by my emphasis on "man." "What if I never got home again, Nors?"

Later that night we sat with a crewman, a steward, looked at dirty pictures of girls, and other things. I'd never seen men with men before—maybe that's why Nors had liked the Navy. From the look on Nors' and the steward's face, the idea wasn't new to them.

I asked if I could leave for awhile. They told me to go up the white ladder that curled to the right. Following their instructions, I'd stepped on one of the catwalks that bordered the boiler room. Nors gave me a book to read–written by Ken Kesey, psychedelic hero of the San Francisco scene.

"Read about his mental hospital escape from the cuckoo straights," Nors suggested. We both knew Kesey was somewhere here in Mexico on the run from the Feds.

"The boilers are really interesting too," Nors added. "They all make different sounds like a bag pipe out of key. Really far out. I'll be there in a minute."

I climbed up an immaculate white, lighthouse-type stairway, onto a similar white-painted platform. My jauraches slapped the hole-filled iron grillwork between the steps, and clanged the metal of the platform.

This is a time to think, I thought, but I could not, and tried to read Nors' book beneath the catwalk leaning against a boiler drum. The boilers whished, screamed and chugged. Its sounds soothed me. I felt like my mother was there. I slept.

A creased hard hand touched my arm.

"Hallo. You." The captain grinned.

I followed him out of the white labyrinth to his cave of small rooms. I entered what seemed to be his living room.

"Stay for a little while. Your friend. He comes up soon." The captain seemed to know what Nors was doing. I didn't like the leer I thought I saw. But he sounded strangely gentle, almost paternal.

A steward brought tea. It tasted good. I wanted to tell the captain about the company I kept, and why.

About my mother, about how I was different from other girls. I couldn't, of course. Not in Greek.

The tea tasted good. It felt good not to be able to talk. The tea tasted like flowers, reminded me of the better times after school when my mother was, almost as a rule, apologetic.

Right this minute on the ship, there was only tea and this hairy fine handsome man, and no talking.

Nors said the girls, the women in On The Road just made it with everybody. It was cool. I wondered if this man wanted that. He seemed to feel sorry for me in a way like my dad. But my dad wouldn't protect me, he was trying to please my mother at all costs. So I'd fled here.

Good riddance, man, I tried to think. My eyes filled with what felt like the white water that lapped down the sides of the ship.

Then a breeze blew over me and my silent captain. We swayed in the hull like two seaweed strands waiting to see if the next wave would entangle us together.

Chapter 11

It didn't. But, in the subsequent days, we were welcomed each morning up the gangplank by the few sailors visible on the huge, empty ship. The ship, white, silver, shining in the sun, invited me as much as the Captain's permission.

I lay in the two-piece I wore all summer, belly flat and brown on the thin white towel over steel near the edge of the starboard side. I looked lovingly at the cerulean water beneath, slapping against the black and silver striped sides.

When I stood, I felt the warm attention of the scattering of sailors, seen and unseen, and the awe of the Japanese on their adjacent ship, lingering leeward to watch Nors—a ruddy Viking albino, and me, walking to the very edge of the top deck and hunkering in position. I sprang off first, arched, and threw myself out into space at the sun. The drop, down three stories, was into hard jeweled spray. Stunned, I circled up from deeper water than I had anticipated, and broke the Japanese-shadowed waters with a smile.

Nors paused above me and hurtled himself, hands and body cutting through first, just his feet clapping the water with a snap.

I dog-paddled down near the ominous sloping iceberg of the Greek ship. Nors whooshed air into his lungs, red-faced, elated, breast stoking with his head up and fully out, found me, and we looked around for the wide spaced black rungs that led upwards. We grabbed hold, climbed tenuously, got over the lowest deck, then scurried to the top, where the captain met us, beaming, easy like the wide abundant sunlight.

When it grew too hot to lie in suits any more, we walked off the ship, out across the long swinging stairway to the dock. Barefoot, I stepped onto the warm wooden sidewalk and slipped into the jauraches.

We threaded back up along the railroad tracks that led from the sea, toward our room that tottered three stories above the tracks. I showered in my suit under the hose head that poured a stream of cold water into the curtainless amber and white peeling closet-like stall. The suit seemed huge in its wet weight. I peeled it off, shook off clear droplets, got out. Nors followed me. I stood in the half-balcony, leaning out over the tracks which veered beneath us at an angle toward the ship.

Bare breasted, nipples taut, skin still kid-smooth and full, I raised two hands and drank in the full sunlight touching crystalline droplets with refracted color.

My strong arched feet on the bare deck, pulsed. Heat dripped back over me like slower, heavier water. It took the droplets up and wrung a slick tropical sweat from me. Still I stood, glistening, on that balcony, feeling like an Andromeda returned to her people.

Caroleena—they could say my name.

Today or any day, Nors and I rarely talked—and that was strange for me. Neither in Spanish nor English, nor my scant French or German, nor even in the six words of Greek we now knew. For me, to talk was to live, to be. But Nors didn't speak much, intent on keeping his on-the-road rhythm. I'd become bonded to him like a child to its mom, leashed to him as a priest of safety. He'd done this before, out of the Navy I guess. I followed him out again in late afternoon, down a labyrinth of narrow steps into the heat-drenched dusk outside the building. He set out swinging his long legs in white bell pants, striking his sandaled feet on the tracks. "Espereme—wait for me," I called.

At the docks we saw it. The ship was gone! It had sailed in the afternoon while he'd slept. Crushed, his Julie Christie face stunned and hurt, he looked at the yawning empty hole left between the Japanese steamer and the clutter of Manzanillo fishing boats, with an almost physical pain, like he'd lost a gleaming tooth. "I knew it'd leave, but later."

That night we paced the courtyard under lantern lights that glowed. The people were so intent on their rituals, chaperoned girls catching sight of young men promenading in clusters to catch sight of them. No one seemed to notice Nors and me, bright burnished oversized summer lobsters caught and spit shells and all, into the center of their town just above the ocean.

"I've heard there's an American resort south of here," Nors pronounced at last. "Maybe I can earn some money. Let's go tomorrow."

I reached for his hand, elated to be able to hold it if I wanted, the way the Mexican girls couldn't. Each look they gave the boys was squeezed out of shy, downcast eyes emanating pain through white slits in the copper dusk. Their looks were so deeply etched, identical. Like racial programming.

Then what about me? I'd brought plenty of programming with me. But I'd set out to be free, and I was.

Solo, I strode now, feeling like the first human to think in this virgin spot. My thoughts rambled, swung back and forth between theories of rigid determinism and solipsistic freedom, like the lanterns swaying regularly on the hot dark breeze.

But there was a scythe, a razor, a layer in the night; like the firelight in the outdoor brazier. I looked into every set of downset feminine eyes I met. I was free, but they weren't.

The next day Nors posed as a preppie at the top of a long wide-paved road ending at a white-tiered resort. I waited in the parking lot. Nors approached patrons walking down toward the few cars parked alongside the hotel. Finally, he connected with an older man and his wife.

"Brown, Brown, wonderful school," I heard Nors shout at the man. After the man withdrew, Nors sprang back gleefully. "He gave me this to clean his car—" Nors waved an imposing stack of American dollars at me.

"He's a Brown alumnus. I was there for a semester before the Navy." Nors straightened up as if he too had an argyle sweater tied over his neck. He asked for a bucket and sponge at the rear of the restaurant.

From wounded men to white resorts. Mexico—land of changing personas. My mind, stilled for a week, had begun to function again.

Nors sloshed soap at the car, returned with buckets of clear water, looked wistfully at the chrome. "Wish I had wax to finish it right." I pulled him away. He dropped his nautical stride, pulled himself to an elegant six feet two, took my arm as if I had just popped over from Bryn Mawr for a game.

Ready after this, for sport of any kind, Nors trolled the long walk from the Brass Slipper Inn, setting his stride toward lone, thatched huts above a long barren beach. "A cafe," he shouted.

Twenty minutes later we slipped into its shadowed three walls and onto stools. "I'm going surfing," he announced after he'd seen someone in a wet suit way out in the waves. I remained at the open-air bar, savoring thatched shadows and the shells thrown over low tables. Sitting here was a brief respite from Nors' choppy vigor.

The inevitable dark, gold-toothed male bartender stared at Nors, clambering down desolate beach into the sea. Nors' height and long yellow hair always confused the Mexican men. My novio, Nors, looked a man and a girl to them.

I saw and heard the sea tug and release me, I sifted in on myself in concentric circles, sat in the sun through thatch brown shadow in a brown land, and looked down at my knees, the darkest they'd been in my life. They weren't really burned anymore but shone like the polished copper pot on my mother's kitchen counter at home, the one she got when she passed from Mamie pink to early American decor. The thatched shadow had lengthened across gilt sands when Nors and a dark, stout—but distinctly American, man—strode up into the open, isolated bar like old friends. The man turned out to be an Italian-American archaeologist out of the University of Florida. He swilled beer and told us we'd stay with him. Our cheesy, penniless grins spurred him on.

We lugged our stuff and his gear back to a dusty Jeep parked behind the "conch shell cafe"—I was going nuts, naming everything, pulled along by some boisterous inner wave.

"One rule I got," the man shouted as we approached his bungalow—one of the lonely ones, so low as to blend with the ground along the road—"No balling when I'm dere, and you don't let no crabs in."

This was an archaeologist? I was insulted until Nors whispered he meant the huge Mexican beach crabs that scratched from the beach at night, crawled up his doorstep and drove him nuts.

"And you gotta go to da whorehouse with me—you're going with me."

What a prodigious sex drive he must have, I speculated. Great. A house of prostitution. Just what I wanted.

I was beginning to like being with Nors and that was enough. I didn't mind at all, being left behind, scuttling crabs and all. Let Nors scuttle, red-bellied, long-legged, up me...

The thought stopped. Like the clarity squinting out of the guilty eyed muchachas promenading around the courtyard in Manzanillo, my own erotic thought was squeezed out by guilt.

We checked out the bungalow. Nors' co-conspirator gave us beer.

Just beneath the surface of consciousness I squeezed out the memory of the new pleasure—the weak, "filthy" answering that had trickled up my thighs when Nors the scuttling crab mounted me—back within, where it would have to live deeper, hidden in the dark recesses of shrouding guilt. To that end I guzzled the whoremaster/archaeologist's copper fluid. The beer brought more autoerotic freedom.

Oh these comes with Nors weren't as powerful as the ones I wrung with my own hands, but I hadn't indulged in a long time. A strange thought occurred—did I sate myself to dissipate the power, to keep the fires low, so that when I touched men, it would be muted, underwater, as though—through a dream?

In the alcoholic warmth, another thought growled up. I want to go to the whorehouse. I felt a randy, low-seated excitement. "Let's go there, Nors."

Our host looked befuddled, surprised, like I'd smacked him.

"Hey, after all, ya don' have to. Whyncha kids stay here."

I flashed back renewed bravado, drumming my fingers on his tabletop. "Let's go, man."

We bounded back into his jeep and bounced through the dark, somewhere, toward another low wall that concealed its little world within.

As we walked around the wall toward its secret opening, I felt all clutched up inside. But the beer slogged and liberated a tough gonadal pull. I strode faster than the men did into the muted lights and low voices. Now I understood Nors' secret—move, it was Kerouac's too; he'd taken his flight from his Mamere, and then became the toughest mama's boy who ever lived. On the road, with no fears but one—it was all action to drown out his inner world.

Move, man, move! Had been the Beats' cry.

It was another three-sided cafe with moldy lanterns, and three ill-matched mariaches starting up, happily thumping, wiping out my errant thoughts. I leaned over the cloth-covered tabletop.

On the far side of the courtyard across a raised outdoor floor I saw other tables laid out in rows.

And I saw a different kind of feminine eyes, glinting, like the slits of the Manzanillo maidens' eyes in rounded downcast faces. But the little bit of life was squeezed out, not in. These shadow women looked out and caught the glances of the men. And I imagined the little glints of life, sex, electricity, dissolving later under greasy embraces, or killed off by the guilt shroud. Whether a female did or didn't, she'd still suffocate beneath it.

I sat, legs spread confidently, jeans soft over sun-warmed skin, buttoned khaki army shirt over my bikini top.

After a while I stood up, left the drumming at the bar and slipped down onto the stone patio, across to my secret sisters in the dark.

I used my best, low-slung slang Spanish.

"What are you doing here?" I asked three plump brown-skinned, glittering-eyed young women sitting on a single bench facing the men across the way. The women looked through me, and away.

"You don't have to do this. You can do what you want." I motioned for a place to sit down. No one moved.

I tried to act loose, asked them where their rooms were. One more mature woman, gold-toothed, black hair burned orangey, waved her hand back over her shoulders. Beads clicked at her neck. She stared up at me with suddenly smart, immovable eyes.

"Get out of here," all the women broadcasted. I stayed, looked into each one of their eyes. There was no light.

The two remaining were more Indian and looked like sisters. Their opaque darknesses flashed back deliberate — I thought — nothingness. I was hurt.

I sauntered back to the men. Their eyes were full of life. Genial. Our Italian/American host patted a chair beside him, patted my head.

"You shudna go out there. You don' know these women, dear."

I brushed his thick hand out of my hair and looked away. I do know, asshole, I wanted to scream.

The place filled up, more men slipped in from the secret opening in the wall.

I drank. I turned my back on the traitors, the women of the night, who rose up and departed to secret rooms one by one, and returned later to the same owl's perch in the dark. Their eyes bored holes into the blackness.

I felt their thoughts glint, white into my back, beaming between my shoulder blades like razors from eyes that weren't supposed to see, that had pulled curtains over themselves when I'd tried to look inside.

The edge of tears folded over my lower lids. I didn't want to be a woman ever again. I looked away from Nors and our whore master host who hadn't budged.

He and Nors seemed connected, mirror image loves, glinting mutual reflections, lighting up the dark like garish neon. And did I detect something else, a low light in Nors' eyes, like I had felt at the concept of whore? I hid imperceptible tears from the enamorators, scraped my chair away and folded, glum, in upon myself.

"Not here, man," another, California man's cool, held-in laugh floated out of far away mariache voices and male murmurs.

"Not any of them. I didn't come for that."

I peeped up. Sure enough. A blond, gaunt, slender chiseled face toked openly on a big number and shrugged his shoulder, and rolled his neck a little like he was performing yoga.

He caught my eye, and left an Americanized Mexican guy alone at the table where he'd been.

Standing over me he asked, "What's happening, chickie?" His eyes sung.

I found out he was from the San Francisco Bay Area too.

"Ken Kesey's here you know," I dropped the name. I'd heard the rumor. He was hiding from the FBI of course.

"You want to come stay with us?" the man challenged.

"With us?"

"Ken and Neal and me. The Merry Pranksters, man, are hiding out."

"Oh. You're here with Ken Kesey?" Sixteen again, I bowed before this courtier to the popular writer/folk idol who'd brought the drug "test" to the San Francisco youth.

I filled Nors in quick.

Nors left the sodden archaeologist alone in the dark, got our things from that man's Jeep and joined us, switching instantly from macho mafioso to hip—it was really amazing.

And we followed the man—his name was Gordon Frazer— back through the secret opening, into the dustiest International four-wheel drive truck I'd ever seen.

Chapter 12

It was a fast, dark drive over unpaved road and sand dunes. Raging through the night, Nors squeezed my thigh. He was going to meet Dean Moriarty, Kerouac's hero of <u>On The Road</u>. In real life, Neal Cassady. I knew what that meant to him.

We disembarked in blackness and the sound of slapping sea. A low-ceilinged house, Mexican/Eichler style, lots of rooms. Apparently, everybody slept. Gordon Frazer led us to a right front bedroom.

"You kin use Mountain Girl's room tonight. She's with... she's with George, man"—our new friend sounded hesitant, like we shouldn't know that—"You'll have to ask her tomorrow."

Left alone in the room, we shied away from the bed where leftover covers intertwined like sweating flesh. We stayed away from someone else's love altar. Instead we unrolled our blanket near a wall and lay still and separate in the buzzing, night heat.

In the morning, the main room filled with racing children,

longhaired men and women. The core group of Merry Pranksters. A woman plunked peanut butter and jelly sandwiches on long tables. The children ate in shifts. She left some for us too. Like we were children. Nors wolfed his—ambrosia.

Afterwards, Mountain Girl—six feet tall, two-toned hair—who just had a baby rumored to be Ken's, even though he had a wife—led us outside toward the Merry Prankster's bus. She didn't explain. We followed her. By now I'd learned her real name was Carolyn Adams, descendent of the presidential Adams.

Outside, Nors jostled my elbow. "Neal Cassady is here someplace!"

In the daylight we could see that The Merry Pranksters occupied two houses separated by a wide expanse of sand. The bus—an old school bus painted with psychedelic swirls—was parked midway, a gathering place. Some days, Gordon had said, the Pranksters made attempts to refurbish it, 3/4 of them stoned at all times.

In the light, Mountain Girl seemed taller than her full-bodied statuesque 6'. She toted her newborn infant daughter to the ocean, bent and dangled towheaded baby Sunshine over the water, her own dyed blonde hair coming in dark at the roots.

She rinsed a wad of brushes at the water's edge, came up on the sand and oversaw the bus painting.

"You kin do this part." She shoved a small brush my way. She didn't even look at me.

I accepted the brush like a scepter. Gordon, shining, handsome, rocked, undulated up close to us, blowing a joint. On the hinge of a sinewy arm he flipped the plump burning number into our faces. Nors slipped his fingers around it and sucked it up between Julie Christie lips, more energetically than I had ever seen anyone suck anything.

He gave it to me, eyes glittering like blue Christmas tree lights with flecks of stroboscopic flash.

Gordon shimmied, a beach man snake. I grabbed the joint and sucked. Left high to paint the bus, life under the brush got ugly. Every stroke became choppy like the cacophonous arrhythmia of my heart. What else was in the Pranksters' pot?

SON JED AND WIFE, FAYE, KESEY

FURTHER

KEN KESEY

NEAL CASSADY

CAROLYN ADAMS - "MOUNTAIN GIRL"

An overly long, metallic two hours later, Mountain Girl came back to scrutinize. I saw her coming, stepped aside. "Who did this?" she barked about the flap behind the front, narrow, passenger-side window. "Look's like a kid did it." She scowled.

Grateful for Mountain Girl's stoned memory loss—she should have remembered it was me—I crouched like a kid, on the bus running board, not saying a thing.

Two men emerged from behind the bus. Mountain Girl hailed them. "Ken, Neal!

"It's too hot to paint anymore now," she stopped us at the men's arrival. "Do it later." The painting project dismissed, she navigated from tall hips on long legs toward a meaty, curly gold-haired man who slipped his arm around her waist.

This must be Kesey.

Nors dropped his brush on the fender. "Did she say Neal, too, man?" he asked me.

"She said Neal."

Blushing, panting, Nors loped toward Mountain Girl and the golden writer hero Kesey. I followed, hidden from Mountain Girl in Nors' shadow.

Nors looked past them for someone else, his eyes falling first upon a clean-cut, black-haired, sky-blue-eyed Lancelot who'd come to join Kesey on his right. Nors looked at me in triumph—he was in love. "Neal Cassady?" He affirmed shyly.

"No," Mountain Girl shook her head. "That's only Babs."

Then a gaunt, grizzled, short 50's hair man who looked to be at least sixty years old—twitching, talking to himself—bobbed and wove out from behind Ken Kesey. I could see why it had taken him a long time to walk a few feet with Kesey. The grizzled man rocked and tremored from the shoulders like someone had held him there and was shaking him out. He tremored toward us and clamped a skeletal hand on Nors' shoulder, quipping, laughing, talking back to himself as he spoke.

"Who's asking?—Who's asking? Har, hah!"

Gordon prodded Nors in the ribs: "Nors, meet Neal—Dean Moriarty from <u>On The Road</u>, to you."

Nors, befuddled, looked from the image of the first, hero-handsome, deep blue-eyed guy on Ken's right, to the bobbing, irritated old man who was everywhere at once.

Gordon, obviously embarrassed in front of Ken, his hero—plunked Nors' butt and pushed him out of the little circle toward the real Neal, who'd released Nors and shook and shuddered in circles around us, making speed-freak mouth noises like the bright weird kid with the briefcase who'd slobbered and said "Beep, beep," to the other boys in line at my junior high school.

"Ooooh!" Nors sucked in his breath and—to his credit—switched dreams, and followed the old man who drew him, vibrating down the beach, jabbing at the air with long bony fingers, flapping leathery elbows, followed Neal Cassady who twisted and spun like the eternal pied piper.

Neal Cassady in loose jeans and worn undershirt, impelled Nors along; Nors who bared his smooth golden chest over rolled-up white Navy-issue pants. Nors looked like an angelic choirboy following the lead of the ferryman into the Underworld—compelled along behind him in untied tennis-shoed feet, into a ghostly realm.

I looked out among the women moving between the Prank-ster's Mexican Eichlers—for someone I could believe in. Mountain Girl was the most revered. She'd just birthed Ken's baby. Faye, his wife of many years and mother of their three children, seemed out of favor, though compensated by her lover George—who appeared to pose in public as Mountain Girl's man. I wasn't on the inside of things, but felt it all. Felt the men clustering around Ken as if to an alpha ape in a primate society where monogamous, noncombative couples weren't found.

In the bungalow, the women washed the dishes, baked the hashish brownies. That night, outside with Ken and Gordon and Nors and Neal and the handsome guy Babs and Zorro and a few others, I asked why this was so. "Why do all the women have to do all the domestic work?"

"It's arbitrary, kid," Gordon quickly defended. "Like, it

could be the people with blue eyes."

Then why isn't it, I wondered.

Ken Kesey got more and more reflective on the opium they were smoking.

"You want some?"

I dragged twice, sure this new terror couldn't be any worse than my fragile experience with Berkeley drugs. Suddenly, lightening flashed in the high dark over the beach. Then thunder, and rain began. We huddled beneath a corrugated overhead that formed a ghostly tin porch.

On the outside of the clique, I caught snatches, in and out, of the high priest and his henchmen.

"Return to the Bay Area? Why not? We will be the new Supermen."

The Superman, same as the Ubermench, the pocket book on Neitsche I'd carried through Mexico all summer had described that. Somehow all roads were trying to lead home. But what were they pointing to?

The next night was a Manzanillo beach version of the San Francisco Fillmore auditorium psychedelic test. Oh my God. That's what I was doing down here in a way, trying to pass the test I'd failed in Berkeley.

In the afternoon they made potent hash brownies. They tasted sweet and innocuous. To belong, I downed a host of them at dinner. They felt safe, nourishing. After all, they were made by women, and these were adults—ten—20 years older than Nors and me, and this was a family.

After this dessert, Zorro led the Pranksters out to the vacant spot between the bus and House #2, and they proceeded to "turn on" and to turn on everybody else in sight. Neal Cassady held out his hand to Nors. On it was piled magic dust.

Gordon Frazer pushed a powdery palm my way. I recoiled. He sensed it. His eyes laughed.

"I've had plenty of hash," I demurred. "Later."

Nors swallowed the powder like Kool Aid or Jello, straight, with an empty, satisfied look, and turned to Ken.

Neal squawked over a loudspeaker. Some music played, waves crashed. The hash began to come on.

I felt and heard an electric buzzing, and from then on, hovered all night, on the edge of a freak out. I found the back flap of the bus in the darkness, and huddled there like a child, hearing huge crabs scuttling across the death-dry sands.

I tried to get back to House #1, where the kids were, and I could sleep, but the attempt made me hideously uneasy, there in the hot, frightening, electric, wired dark. There were no friends, only strangers. I was too pumped up and far away from the equal hideousness of the ugly nest of home, to cry for it. Sometimes the mind compresses in memory what it elongates at the time. Sometimes, the mind protects. I only vaguely remember getting to the house somehow, and Gordon Frazer, kinder now, handing me another pill, this time a tranquilizer, and I slept.

The next day Ken decided the men would go to Mexico City for some reason, so it was possible for Nors and me to hitch a ride. Summer was ending. And Nors had sprung something new—about meeting his mother. And after that, one of these days, I would have to fly home.

We piled in the dusty International, stopped somewhere on a mountain pass and slept in a cooler dark. Ken and the guys took the comfortable back seat and Nors and I were left the front seat, and finally climbed onto the flat roof and lay, clammy in the jungle mist, until morning.

In Mexico City they left us off fast, dragging away as soon as Nors' rucksack was off the tailgate. Still befuddled from the hash and tranquilizer, I forgot for a split second that my passport was on the front seat. But it was too late—they were gone.

Chapter 13

Since his first "trip", Nors wasn't Nors any more. He couldn't help with practicalities like passports. The psychedelic drugs had opened a new door, and he stood there staring through it—and after Neal Cassady who'd just gone out of his life.

Nors and I spent the next days in Mexico seeking help from the native student we'd met during the summer session. It helped to know Ariel Zuniga. Son of a sculptor, grandson of a great revolutionary. Wading through the unfamiliar bureaucracy, we waited each day in empty stucco buildings until my papers could be reproduced. Thanks to Ariel, they could be, but it took many days.

On the last day of waiting I sat dejected and mindblown in the Officina de Gobierno. Ariel Zuniga, almost the only Mexican man who hadn't spit at me in one way or another, almost the only man I'd spent any time with at all, that I hadn't also touched, approached me. Thinking of this, I was embarrassed when he said he wanted to present me with something.

"I have to speak to you...por favor, it's only for a moment, but it is of the utmost importance."

With ceremonial flourish, Ariel presented me with a thick stack of half-sheet size, printed leaflets.

Impatient to avoid his gaze, I took the papers and read: "LUCHA PARA LAS MUJERES." Rights for the women of Mexico. Radical socialism could free them from the double standard, either prostitute or domestic prisoner. For a moment, it greatly appealed. Ariel, big, dark, over-serious dogface, bent in anticipation. I could see he cared for me.

"Will you stay, and lead this?" he asked, big soft brown eyes tunneling into mine.

Filled with self-disgust, I couldn't meet his eyes. Kesey cool nearly took me over. I almost said, so Ariel you work in a factory while you go to school—to be what—one of the people, a worker—so what? You're just Ariel, sculptor's son. Why don't you go home and turn on?

Instead, in the only truly good act I'd ever committed in Mexico, I held his sweaty, puffy, paw hand and lowered my eyes in deep respect.

"Such a deep honor, Ariel. I cannot—now. But thank you, my friend."

Ariel withdrew his hand, covering his eighteen-year-old boy feeling with communist valor and indifference. "It matters not what you say—what part any of us may play—the Struggle will continue—we are...as insignificant."

"And perhaps, someday, Ariel—maybe someday, I will help bring luchas para las mujeres." Then I told him I loved him, choosing the right Spanish form that meant "friend".

He smiled, eyes wet, and shuffled back inside to hurry somebody or the other up. Then I did something I'd never done in Mexico—I allowed myself to cry.

The afternoon rain began in quick showers. Pelted by horse droplets I cried from low down, from a deeper source than I could yet understand.

A leaflet he'd dropped curled up at my feet. Water ran over the homemade ink in LUCHAS and it trickled over PARA and like long hair, obscured MUJERES. Luchas. Rights.

Sunlight reappeared and the rain sloshed through it between shrubbery. I remembered the lightening streaking down the beach at Manzanillo while the Merry Prankster men, as Ubermensch, plotted their San Francisco Bay Area return. I saw Ken Kesey then as Neitsche—Neitsche who'd hitched a woman psychologist to a dogcart. I'd read that was Nietsche's idea of woman's contribution—"bearing" the Super race.

Rights. Oh good, good Ariel—he still had the feeling I'd begun with. What had started in Berkeley, peace, civil rights, a call to march, had culminated in psychedelics, opium, hash, male privilege and disillusion in the depths of Mexico.

I waited out the last week before my flight back, in a three-story house in the downtown. Nors and his mom were ensconced in two beds in one motel room nearby. Shady fronds and thick carpets quieted Nors and his mothers' voices when I went to visit. I thought of Jack Kerouac and wondered how he felt when he retreated to his Memere.

At the motel room, I'd sat on Nors' bed. His mother murmured from the bath, "We'll have to find you somewhere else to say. I know these people in the downtown."

Nors and his blonde Mama had rushed me though Mexico City to my new abode. "I'll see you when we get back," he whispered.

In my new house there was a newlywed couple—the girl dark-haired, the man boyish, lanky, sprinting off here and there. She was like an adoring mother to her new husband when she described an ecstatic acid experience—his—they'd shared at Yosemite National Park. "When the acid peaked," she gushed, proud and excited like a parent whose boy had just made Eagle Scout, "when the rush came, he climbed behind Bridle Veil Falls with an erection." She pursed the word giddy sweet—"e-rec-shun".

I saw it, hard and wet, an arrow the brave boy hunter accompanied on its flight into life, and the laughing acid mother wife, triumphant, his opportunity to be an eternal boy, springing from her unselfishness.

The young wife Dora made sandwiches in the drafty kitchen of a house that could have been any in Berkeley. "Where did you get white bread?" I asked.

"Tony likes it," Dora said. Abracadabra. Tony likes it. It appears. I wanted to go home. I also wanted a home to go to. Abracadabra.

One morning waiting I left them in the kitchen of their house on Istacihuatl Street. I trudged up narrow stairs to the third floor where I slept, and around the corner from the bedroom put my towel on the clawfooted bathtub. I stripped.

In the mirror, I looked thinner than I had ever remembered myself, hipbones defined. I was dismayed, for some reason, at the size of my hips—wouldn't they go away by now? They were narrower than my shoulders, but still widened into a classic Grecian curve.

Dora, the young wife, had given me kitchen matches to light this upstairs water heater. I tugged open an engraved iron door at the bottom of the thick white heater. Brown rivulet water stains ran lower down it like light brown hair. I crouched naked, head bent, lit the match. The heater exploded.

Ejected out of the bathroom, I collapsed on the cold blue tile and smacked my head. I rubbed my head, singed eyebrows and smoking hair.

Shaken, I struggled into my dirty clothes and returned downstairs to Dora. Tony was back, toking up on a thick little phallus-shaped joint. I wove toward them.

"What happened to you, kid?" he asked.

"The heater blew up." I brushed my newly frizzed hair back from my eyes with cool aplomb.

"Gee Tony, she looks terrible," Dora remarked.

"Want some?" Tony held up his joint.

I'd never joined in with them before. Escaping acid with Kesey had worn me down. I saw the challenge in his eye.

Dora had her arm around my waist. Now Tony and I were both her babies. I grabbed Tony's joint with expertise and toked deep. I didn't let the breath go until my lungs exploded for air.

In three minutes I felt the rush begin. Blood went out of my face. This was no grass!

Tony swung out of the kitchen with a white bread sandwich, went down the back steps and out. Didn't Dora care where Tony went on weed? My blood rushed back up and held like an airplane, suspended for a sickening moment between trajectory and light. Oh God! Not again. Dora, Dora.

I couldn't even think of Tony, off, up in his pants no doubt, and what the son of a bitch would say if Dora told him I'd "freaked out".

"Dora..."

"What's the matter, babe?"

"The explosion. My ears are ringing." I, who had escaped that easier, water heater cataclysm, lied. It wasn't cool to tell the truth—I couldn't take their grass.

"Oh, I don't know what to do, doesn't the weed relax you, babes?"

It did not. The internal airplane screamed, inside turbine engines blown off, the other imploding on the passenger's inside.

"Oh, a little. You got anything else?" From far away fear I still tried to sound like a cool, dumb hippie.

"I got a Thorazine." She fished inside her apron pocket. "Tony makes me keep these in case he needs one."

"Tony?" I gurgled. Who was he? I was spinning, dying, needed help fast.

"Here. Take it, babes."

I gobbled the thing and ran upstairs. The sidewalls loomed elongated, every scratch, every dead insect magnified. The dust going up was a numbing wind tunnel—a trip down the Moffett Field blimp hanger back home.

"Please. Work," I cried to the wall in a thin voice.

The pill caught me at the top of a fast twenty-minute trip up the labyrinth stairs and I began to slow down. Peace, like a ship, radiating light through a thick fog on Manzanillo Bay, slid closer to me. The cells of my body reached out for it. I slowly strapped on my juaraches, grabbed a woven rainbow bag and swam through the dark and light opaque waters down the stairs toward the kitchen.

"I'm going out, Dora," I said.

"OK, babes?"

"OK"

Taking a wad of poison I'd popped out of their American hippie house into the din of Mexico City, I was a gringa weaving through the blinding white market place light of the noonday sun.

I bought mangos, a platina from the stall a half block down, then slid around the corner for pan dulces. I murmured to the dueno of the pandulceria, patted a peso on the counter in slow motion, stuffed the bag of frosted sweets back into my bag.

Now I was moving even more slowly. The sun baked each one of the sweet breads popping out of the bag I gripped by one handle. To lift my knee, shin, then foot, over the curbside coming out of the street was a deep, sleepy labor. As though I'd been hit by a hammer, I reeled slowly in the direction I apprehended might be right.

Christ. There must be a Christ. This time no greasy brown sunglassed male with poor dental work hissed "puta" after me, nor "chee chee", nor "mami" like the deranged insects they were.

There was the house. I peered up a million miles, up the one step from street to kitchen. I fell against the door.

Inside it was cool. Tony'd come home to mama Dora for his afternoon snack. Dora took my arm and led me up the stairs where I didn't care whether Tony thought I was "uncool, man," or not.

I fell asleep, dreamed of Frederich Nietsche with a white bread sandwich and an erection, Tony on Thorazine and me, tied to a dogcart on Istacihuatl Street. I crawled around on my knees, nosing the gutter, looking for a Western Airlines ticket amongst spit and soggy pan dulces. The dream scene shifted to Dora, weaving from the upstairs window of the Ixtacihuatl house, her eyes brimming with slow blue tears as if she had downed all the Thorazine in her apron pocket at once.

I snapped awake, but the Thorazine knocked me back down into my bare mattress and ragged dreams.

A week later I flew home on an airplane above the glowing orb of the sun, and at the San Francisco Airport, climbed up the high steps of the Greyhound bus.

Chapter 14

Berkeley

It was fall. I ran, tore down Telegraph Avenue. After several weeks of not hearing from Nors I'd called his mother's place on the Berkeley/Oakland border.

In Berkeley now I ran, in golden yellow corduroy pants and an orange sweater, ran down Telegraph Avenue at break neck speed, hair flying out behind me. At the University gate, a man with a beard caught up to me.

"I've been watching you," he said with eyes that looked like he was on a trip. "You're the only young person here."

Since the new slogan was, "Don't trust anybody over thirty," that was a big complement. Of course, I was only seventeen. I smiled, pacing at the signal, in a hurry, waiting for the light to change.

He stared in adulation. It wasn't odd for strangers on trips to make cosmic connections. "You can come too..."

He looked sorrowful. "I didn't mean that."

He'd taken it wrong—thought I was responding to an advance. I felt bad—I didn't want to interrupt his vision. But when the light turned green, I tore through the clot of students and streaked off down Ashby like a flame.

When I arrived at Nors' mothers' place, he didn't let me in, greeting me from a closed porch instead. It was a small pretty house, white frame and glass—I could see potted plants behind him. He opened the screen and popped down a few steps.

I looked up into his blue eyes, idealizing now, every moment we'd spent together this last summer in Mexico. He let me leap up against him like a sun-burnished setter. He laughed, and lifted me for a moment.

Behind him a young woman who looked like a figureless kid, emerged. This was the hometown girl he had mentioned. Sort of a relative. I paid little attention.

After some conversation with this Sissy, who looked twelve and unformed although she was a year older than I was, Nors and I left to meet my friend Olive at her Berkeley art student pad. Sissy couldn't come along, she wanted to wait for Nors' mother.

We skipped up the street. "Hold on now," Nors panted. "I just had a hit, and it's about to come on."

A hit. The drug.

Tying to pass Kesey's test, I'd done it again when I got back, taken some stuff in the Big Sur woods with Mak. Before hand, someone gave me a huge bag of the Librium I'd gotten from Gordon in Mexico. As soon as the stuff came on, even in the redwood trees, it was a replay of the worst of that first time on the Berkeley campus.

The second time had brought back the first. From the elastic beginning of that time on campus, with couples like protons and electrons revolving around each other and the sense of an impending cataclysm, to taking more of it, seeing a third eye in the center of Karl's forehead; we must have been huddled like lovers on the grass—the police had made us move, somehow we'd gotten across the world to crouch in terror on stone benches in the surreal world outside Sproul hall.

There the cosmic ugliness set in—the sun hit the concrete, flowers seemed stuck in dry dirt like dead sticks, there I heard the drag of a crippled woman's foot, scraping, scraping in the interminable toil of her walking.

I'd returned to hell the second time in Big Sur, first the terror rocket in my chest. Then Mak grew fangs, his hands were claws, he called me the Madonna, I was in hell. Insects like 'Nam helicopters assaulted me and I downed the bag of huge looking green and white capsules. Only hours later did I come to, somewhere down the forest trail on my back, parts of my memory for months of my life gone, a strange little straggly-bearded man over me holding out an acorn that grew into a tree in his hazy hand.

Here today in Berkeley, at every other step I took with Nors, fear lurched in me between radiant giddiness. When we got to Olive's I could sense envy behind her dark, solemn productive Jewish analysis of everything. Today to her, Nors and I were the epitome of blithe wasp ways—of irresponsible freedom. We slipped away to her back porch where I was bedding. We closed the door and got under a comforter tied with yarn Olive had spun last winter.

The windows were steamed above where we lay between the washer and dryer into a cedar-walled corner blocked from outside view.

Nors began to kiss me up my throat, plush lips behind my ears. He grabbed my breast to steady himself tight. He shimmied out of his navy wool bell-bottom sailor's pants and regarded me in his white underwear.

It never ceased to amaze me that Nors had kept his clothes so neat in Mexico. Today his shorts fairly gleamed—his mother's additional touch, I guessed.

His penis, long and visibly trembling, aimed at me in the space between us. I took it, stroked it toward me between Mexican bought abalone and silver ringed fingers.

He twisted the tip to find room, and screwed it into me.

After the moment of penetration that always snapped my

101

breath, and before the first stroke, I remembered—he was on acid.

I turned my face away toward the washer so he could not find my lips. He began, the sailor's distant rhythm, bodies not touching. Now I knew why I longed for more in Mexico. He titillated my nether lips, but refrained from the deepness that teased a woman's sensitive outer organ to orgasm. It begged to be touched deeper. The pull of his twisting screwing penis, the pressure of his thighs, the golden, arching movement of his boy's shanks, almost did it.

It was maddening. I contracted my cervix in imagination. I didn't want any acid-permeated sperm to enter. Maybe it wasn't imagination.

"Oooh, oooh," he sang through his full beautiful Julie C. lips, and the fearful pressure of my athletic vaginal muscles that milked out every creamy, acid-soaked drop. Afraid at that thought, I got up right away, naked before the steamed-up windows, and let his fluid eke down my thigh.

While doing this, I laughed, trying to remain cool. It was good to see Nors. But I was restless with tension.

Nors' eyes glittered like his shiny navy buttons. He was "peaking" now.

Olive tapped on the glass panel of the redwood shake door. Architect Julia Morgan had made these places long ago, all redwood shake, all Berkeley. I got up, clean towel grabbed from Olive's laundry wrapped around me. I could see only Olive's dark eyes and the top of her sinewy black hair—she was so short.

"Mak's here." My neighborhood friend emerged from around Olive. Curly brown hair, nice eyes, weak chin, ideal body. Mak my pot mentor.

The boy who's poetry and acting I adulated, who's prick I first stroked, but—referencing my own female anatomy, got it upside down. Now he followed me, to meet my friends. "You've got to meet this guy Nors," I'd told Mak when I'd gotten home. "He can tell you about Kesey and the electric kool aid acid test."

Today Mak ambled in, covering his chin as he always did,

in bitter self-consciousness. He was growing a scrawny beard on it now, and pulled on these wisps in the manner of a Chinese grandfather.

Nors blurted out, "Hi, man—now I get it."

"He's stoned," I whispered to Mak, who watched with the hollow open eyes he used to suck in the inspiration for the poems he wrote. Lawrence Ferlinghetti's City Lights had just recognized the light I'd seen in Mak's poems written on scraps of brown paper bags, when I was thirteen. He was published!

Nors continued his drug-induced insights. "She's—she's— woman." Nors pointed at me. Mak nodded, apprehending some- how. As always I puffed out with somebody else's positive vision of me, smiled gracefully, instantly in character.

"And you, man, you're really a man." Mak's broad shoul- ders and sagaciousness became the masculine archetype. Olive knit her brows; she didn't seem to have the knack of stepping into somebody else's vision. She looked like she might laugh. But our Aryan chutzpah held her back.

"But me, I'm neither, really. Like Sissy–you saw her. We're really in between, androgynous, a man and a woman both, you see." And he smiled up at Mak, bright blue eyes glowing and proud. Mak made some clever non-remark that left him free of ridicule.

Olive asked, "Who wants spaghetti? I think I have enough. I'm going to need more money for the sourdough and dressing though. Why don't you come with me to the store, Colly?"

Caught in the swirl of two men, and basking in their respect for each other, I was at the apex of a very happy triangle.

"Sure, sure, Olive, I'll come." But I thought Olive was out of it. Forgetting that Olive had an IQ of 150, that unbelievable score being higher than either of these men, I thought her forgivably petty and uncool, today. We trotted off to the store, an old familiar pair. Later over dinner there was comfort in pouring the Girard's pyra- mid-shaped bottle of dressing I'd bought, in shaking the seasonings at the bottom and watching herbs float down like the snowflakes from a Christmas past. That was psychedelic enough for me.

Chapter 15

Palo Alto

Back at home for high school of all things, I still liked to be outside. Outside it was clear, heady and objective. I often got away, ran away, lied away, broke away and arranged to be away, pacing up Middlefield from Menlo Park.

I'd still bound past Willow Road with its grill that made the delicious hamburgers my dad had liked—meaty ones with pickles and onions and mustard. I'd still cut to the right and wind around the San Francisquito Creek—the historic dividing line between Menlo Park saloons and Stanford University. The creek was little and deep with foliage Mak and I had once hidden in, pockets of wild mystery.

On those earlier high school days when Mak, now a drop-out and dope smoker and poetry writer—had persuaded me to join him, we'd light up in the wilds of the creek. Then Mak had stared with a leering smile all the time, covering his self-hatred with cool. Then we'd ambled along the creek together. His dark curls had gleamed in a different way than my long hair tangling and blowing free in my face. We scrambled up and down the creek embankment or walked along its pathway, depending upon whether there were houses abutting it.

Clambering along behind him, I'd ignored my mother's admonitions. "Mak was a muskrat, he sniffed after girls," she'd said. I wasn't the only one—my Standard Oil heiress friend escaped having his child in high school, one "older" woman agonized too long but had an abortion anyway. Finally a Catholic woman gave birth to his son in an apartment by the freeway.

But even by that time Mak wasn't as interested in me as sexual prey, as he was in the luminous pathways of experience opened to him by grass highs.

And these days, with Ferlinghetti's recognizing him, publishing his poetry the high school teacher called "schizophrenic", he could quit high school and write. But months had passed since the publication of those three little poems, and he was middle class like the rest of us. Out of school, his dad said he'd have to earn money from poems or go to work at the family's concrete firm—the end of his life's ambitions. His dad's pressure drove him back to the dreamy influence of weed.

I too, former Jr. High Valedictorian, aspirant to the class presidency until I'd heard "Girls don't run for that", had also cut school and wandered in this creek.

Returned from Mexico to the end of high school, I still straggled into classes that humiliated me. The same icy, better-than-average, precocious group of gifted kids I'd come up with, only tolerated my "cool" remarks I used to cover up skipping class and not knowing the books.

Sometimes I caught a special glimmer in a perceptive instructor's eye, including that Negro teacher who invited me to a multiracial weekend group from poorer schools, talking about the S.A.T. But inside, the weight of sweaty, ill-prepared failure at Menlo-Atherton tugged me down, and I felt as psychedelically self-conscious as Mak.

Still I coursed through classes irregularly, like the water in the creek, in tiny trickly increments, or in tremorous gushes; I earned an average of "B's" in the things that I liked. But that was a heartbreak. I knew I should have had straight A's and been president of the senior class. Maybe in a way I was—certainly as a vanguard. In Menlo Park in 1967, "hippies" didn't exist. I was the only student in the graduating class who'd raised money for black voter registration, been tear gassed in front of the Oakland Induction Center, stayed with Kesey, been offered leadership of the campaign for Lucha Para Las Mujeres—Rights For Women In Mexico, and written significant poetry on mostly lost paper bags—published in the school literary magazine.

Three months before graduation–drug shaken–in the girls'' gym, sweaty, ill-prepared for badminton, I saw all of them staring at me. A cacophony of stares from all their unforgiving years of staring at me, rose up in my blood like a strange dose of the Drug, and I grappled to the door through a sea of surrealistic faces. Once outside, I blacked out over the concrete drinking fountain, I came to and walked home.

After that incident, I went to a non-communicative Rogerian therapist I'd already found, to deal with the Drug effects. He said, about helping me finish high school with a home tutor, "I don't want to institute a pattern of this"—but I looked so shaken, he wrote a letter. So I got the home tutor for the last three months, and finished up, commuting between Tupper's Park—the last days I'd ever be there—and Palo Alto's Lytton or Channing, hippie crash houses that had become my milieu. Not only had I been to Mexico, known Kesey, but also I'd had my passport returned by Kesey's henchman Gordon Frazer. I belonged.

In Palo Alto on one of those days, my friends Heather May Beck and Frannie Jinx and I strolled out of Lytton house joyfully under the nose of the Palo Alto police station a half block over, going toward the downtown. I spun around to look back up at the cupola and Heather May's three story Victorian rented tower room. We were into Victorian and 40's and bohemian costumes. Jinx wore a St. Vincent De Paul fur jacket with round-toed, red forties shoes, hose over unshaven legs and a shoulder-padded dress. This was 1967. Way before all that stuff would been revived—she was just thinking it up.

I wore a ribbed horizontal striped velour shirt—neither was velour the "in" thing—and cords, over high moccasins through which I could feel the cool concrete as I walked.

Heather May had on pants with a little flair at the bottom, and a long Victorian blouse that buttoned, and boots, too—crisp leather shiny ones. Today she also wore a British cap and a Sergeant Pepper jacket. In warmer weather she wore the triangular scarves with dangling fringe that Jinx had picked up when we'd gone thrifting.

Nobody could find the beautiful things Jinx could. She had an eye for old classic fabrics—instilled in her by her east coast dowager grandmother's tastes from thirty-five years earlier. Raised by this crabby, taciturn woman and at Swiss boarding schools while her mother made her way through her State Department career, Fannie Jinx Smythe had interjected odd bits and pieces of her grandmother. So she spat back piss and vinegar at the oddest times. She was choppy, spare and unforgiving of herself, disciplined in this undisciplined lifestyle we all led, and, as one passing lover had remarked, "compulsively honest".

I'd first met Jinx when she was washing her Borgward car on the front lawn of a Palo Alto house—capable and independent. She even rebuilt the motor. A different kind of woman. I looked up to her at the start, and never stopped.

108

I emulated what she knew, took up drawing for example. We'd sketch each other, drag in anyone we could find. Guys, usually. Made 'em strip down in exchange for some food she "bagged" when the checkers weren't looking.

She'd buy a cheap item, celery, say, stuff a packet of fresh crab in her bag, and voila, crab salad and all the male nudes we needed. In my estimation, she could do anything. She was always six years older than I, and that helped. Next month she would be twenty-three.

Heather May was two and a half years older, and had the right to live away from her home and hip family and all, so in some ways I looked up to her too. But in other ways Heather May was the same beloved baby with us that she was with her hip sister and brother-in-law.

With page boy dark blonde hair, full figure and dangling bracelets, Heather May exuded femininity and sweetness that somehow weren't contradicted by her love habits, including sleeping with the irascible old Neal Cassady, folk hero to the beats and Nors' introduction to "The Drug" in Mexico. I'd invited Nors to Palo Alto, told him about Jinx and Heather May and about Heather May sometimes sleeping with his hero Neal Cassady.

If Heather May wanted to lie on her mattress after our nude drawing sessions, go back upstairs with this "old man", Cassady, it was cool. Though young, she had the nurturing motherly quality that softened her liaisons and made them— sweet.

We three friends just fell in where we were. Me at just seventeen, the still furtive high school refugee and world traveler. And Heather May and Jinx. That day, we variously padded, clipped and clopped, up Lytton Avenue to University, free as the proverbial breeze.

On a gray, overcast dawn a week later, I crept down from the upstairs bedroom in the Lytton house tower and set out, head bowed, through the streets for the bus station at the end of University Avenue. I walked down the tunnel inscribed with graffiti and peopled with the disconsolate as if I belonged to their company.

Last night my beloved, flashy Nors, had pulled into Palo Alto late, and had strutted from the bus station to Lytton House. He and I had clambered to the third, attic, room, where Heather May Beck, one of my best friends, slept in the tower dome she'd draped so tastefully with India plaid. When we got up in the cupola, her roach clip and her beads lay beside her.

She was alone. She stirred in the semi-dark, and reached a plump, delicate Art Nouveau hand for the lamp switch. Her light bracelets had clanged together.

She shook her page boy blonde hair and smiled from a cupid bow mouth. "Nors." She'd giggled seductively, "Colly's mentioned you to me."

He took it in, this mother loving, I will belong to no woman guy. "Don't get up. May we sleep here?" He asked. Somehow, amid further giggling, he was in the middle of the two of us.

Heather May had cut out the light and lit a candle.

Nors brought out some stuff he had. Heather May and Nors used Heather's clip until it only held an ember. They sucked at the red dot of fire.

Nors blew out this light too. "Goodnight."

There was much murmuring, getting comfortable, then a yearning silence. Nors, who had turned coldly away from me, began to work on Heather May. Heather's pot-soaked breathing was clearly audible in the little bed. Nors patted my knee once or twice, perfunctorily as he jockeyed closer into position by Heather May.

They were stoned, I wasn't, and this was all going on. In the dark, I had miserable time to think. Tonight, Vis a Vis Nors' Berkeley psychedelic vision of archetypes, was I the kid, and Heather May—Woman, and he at last, Man?

I'd often thought Heather May, Frannie Jinx and I were like three visions of woman in sequence: Frannie Jinx, slim-hipped, and though shorter, muscular, small-breasted and randy; myself the tallest, long-limbed, breasts described as a perfect handful; Heather May medium height, full-breasted, full-hipped—the most estrogenic of us, perhaps.

At the hot baths in Big Sur once I had inadvertently insulted

Heather May, who was on acid at the time and impressionable. I'd told the story of a large-breasted girl I'd known from high school, who'd run off with the Gypsy Jokers bikers group. "Her breasts were like cysts," I'd said, for some reason contemptuous.

That day in the Big Sur woods Heather May had told me I'd made her self-conscious, like her breasts were "cysts" and too large. I'd said that day I was truly sorry, but, if it could be admitted, I admired Jinx' body far more than Heather May's.

But Heather May fit, and acted, an image that some men found attractive. I heard more sounds. Was this lovemaking with Nors, her revenge for that dumb comment about Letty Underwire, the Joker's mama? Lying next to Nors' and Heather May's submerged coupling sounds, I didn't know. But I'd stumbled into my clothes in the dark, feeling wildly desolate and glad to get out of that cloying tower room overladen with Heather May's musk incense. Barefoot, I'd stepped on Heather's sharp amethyst beads lying below the bed. Usually careful and neat, Heather May would, under other circumstances, have minded the little crunch, and sweetly retrieved them.

But last night she'd just kept on with whatever she was doing with Nors. I'd pressed out of my mind the easy suggestion of amber limbs, yellow look-alike hairdos and the sweet surrender—that was phony, I well knew—to Nors's plunging. That he never pressed close enough, as he despised "that", seemed to pale from my thoughts.

Out of the tower room last night, away from Nors and Heather May together, well up the streets from Lytton house, I'd staggered down the narrow, curvy "secret stairway" I usually liked to climb, hurt to the core, feeling as blackly alone as the hobos I caught leaning under the illustrious Stanford overpass.

I'd walked 'till five thirty a.m., gotten a doughnut and coffee from one of the few working people's cafes in Palo Alto. At least there were some then, not cloyed with look-alike Roots shoe stores and earth food restaurants and self-conscious bookstores, like later. Then it was vital and open.

In '67 Palo Alto was still real enough to allow me to be an

111

anomaly at 5:45 A.M.—a seventeen-year-old girl trudging upward to the bus station nestled in the crooked arm of University Avenue before it turned toward the great school. The station then was a shelter for the outcasts of the moment, for those who didn't seem to fit anywhere.

Through the tunnel, the dawning air was damp to breathe. The swish of a few headlighted cars around the circle to the terminal gave brief respite to the salmon gray rising light.

I wriggled my toes in my Mexican summer's juaraches and smiled Nors' cheesy rubelita's smile. I fought for a strong, angry thought. That it would be awhile before I trusted him, was too weak.

Underneath it all I really knew, hands in my cracked, Mexico-stained amber pocket, that it was finished for Nors and me. I even wondered if he had used this cruel medium to disentangle himself from me and the discomfort I caused his mother.

They're—all of them—these guys, phonies, I said to myself, sounding real hip. But it was true, I was beginning to know the story. At seventeen, alone at 6:13 A.M., I felt a lot freer than Kerouac at age thirty, bouncing home to his mother's way of thinking.

And in another way it felt good to be back at the bus station, looking at the smelly bums like wizened old rats, out of my own eyes, like when I'd first come to Olive's in Berkeley. It was important to look out of my own eyes, not anybody else's.

And birds still tweeted in the shrubbery around the Palo Alto station. In fact, a flock of bigger birds swirled above my head and flipped toward the south. The birds looked like one of Heather May's jeweled nineteenth century thrift shop scarves—but shaken out, all the black birds like onyx beads, freed out of formation and scattered across the sky.

That Heather May's sister told her later friendship was more important than guys, still left me on my own again.

I convinced my parents to let me rent a cheap room at an art studio. There's home guys like Mak and downtown guys like the older hipsters, looked to hang out with me at all hours, I didn't want to be uncool. After awhile the owner needed the front room for display. I moved to a back garage. Kesey's compatriot Gordon Frazer got wind of this, and followed me all the more.

One weekday afternoon when there was no home tutor, I sat atop Gordon Frazer. "Chicks like this." Gordon lay back in the loft of the garage he had stolen from me for his own. He reached over his head for a chocolate-covered cherry from a box hidden behind his pillow—"our" pillow.

We had everything here, food, a freestanding, black, cast iron wood stove in the garage I had been offered when Paul needed the front lower room I'd rented virtually free—part of his plan to expand Cowper house into a gallery. And now Gordon had appropriated the garage from me.

Gordon sucked at the chocolate-covered cherry. His teeth clicked. Later Heather May told me with her post-adolescent giggle, "They're fake." She'd slept with him too.

Gordon, a wise, wizened 29 at least, swiveled his thin hips only slightly. I did almost all the swiveling, liking the feeling, rubbing when I wanted to, liking the feather light drag of mons against his pubis. In the semidarkness I could hide the feelings of real, though mild, genital pleasure. Gordon smacked his chocolate-covered lips and whistled a tune from that repertoire collected for his only purpose—to sound cool.

He often squeezed his shoulder blades together in response to questions—like when I'd ask if the garage was his, or still mine at all—he'd scrunch his shoulders and say, "That's trips."

"What, Gordon?"

"That's trips." He'd rock, lifting his shoulders to his ears.

"Why are you doing that?" I'd ask.

"Because I wanna." He'd grin his elfin smile and lean one hand proprietarily on a beam of his garage. "That's trips."

"Gordon why do you do that? We're talking."

"You can do it too, do it anytime, like this, and people will think you're cool, man. That's all—that's trips." He seemed glad to be the sagacious, shoulder-lifting instructor of cool.

"Far out," I'd finally agreed.

But after these inane lessons, I had something over on

Gordon, although I was convinced he knew—when supine—what he was doing. He produced these sensations in me effortlessly, because he was so cool.

But...ooh they felt good. When so engaged, he liked my black turtleneck lifted up a little—it was cool in here. He played with my breasts. Then he'd dropped his hands, and lain still, a shadow of cool in the subdued fire-mounting dark.

And I'd try to pace myself to his controlled rhythm... I was a hungry tigress cub.

The little ripple of orgasm that squeezed out between the planes of our tongue and groove loins, bubbled up and pawed through the chestnut-colored hair of my snatch, as Gordon too called my feminine center.

Again. I wanted to try again. And Gordon didn't stop, he only slowed his movements. The sting and the numbness of "just after" passed, then the itchy, gathering sensation. Even if it wasn't a mature woman's force out of the tip, hot red, erect, and then the light inner, ecstatic, orgiastic clutching, it was at least another step in learning with a man.

Wow. That was almost as good, I thought, as myself—not quite, not quite at all, but nearly. I didn't like Gordon, but made myself think I did. After these sessions he would prop himself and sit up to enjoy more chocolate-covered cherries.

His otherwise nondescript penis sat up, droozly in his lap. Neat, I thought, the way it collapsed in that straight up position like one of those three piece camp cups that compressed down into two or three inches.

Gordon was heading for an early death from a drug overdose. He'd turned my good friend Nors onto acid, he'd taken my garage. Still, Gordon showed me one thing "that chicks like" and also how to squeeze my shoulders together to look cool. I rarely do it, I mean I never do it. It would be nice if I did sometimes, because it's sad that a man could leave nothing of himself behind that anyone would want to imitate.

Chapter 16

Big Sur: Esalen Baths

At dusk on the hill at Big Sur that spring, we gathered about the firelights. I guess it should have been some kind of celebration. The Negro instructor who made me take S.A.T.'s and apply for Berkeley was right, they wanted me, I didn't tell my friends here, they didn't care about school, and people and places like these had taught me the most.

The cool dug shadows on the mountaintop. Pale blue keyholes opened in the gray and pink and white clouds.

Harry, who ran St. Michael's Alley, older, with glasses, was Jinx's latest consort. She'd brought us here, my leach friend Paul Beannie—who'd rescued me on that other bad trip in the Big Sur woods when I'd come back from Mexico, and Heather May and her new macrobiotic Stanford boyfriend Leon and Heather's gay confident Blade, to the top of a dark bluff above the campgrounds miles inland from the ocean.

Harry's dog yapped behind his heels, then settled, when he hunched down in boots over a big, crackling fire. Jinx hunched beside him, short, Irish-brown hair swinging and shiny, glasses periodically pushed back up on the bridge of her nose. She wore a loose, ripply, India blouse, itself an unusual mauve toward purple color pleating out from the yoke over her small jutting breasts.

She dug her bare toes over the tip of her sandals and into the dust. The rest of us hunkered around the fire. After awhile Heather May reclined like the lady she was—against Leon who'd anticipated her movements and had seated himself as a backrest for her against the dirt.

Little firefly stars spit out from between the heavy clouds, a gauzy cloth backlit with dust blue luminous patches.

The dark closed around us. There were no car sounds, no isolated shouts, no airplane engines.

We settled into the night. If there was anything I learned from them, it was to go with the flow.

Wind, dark, energizing, from an indeterminable place, whirled around us like a sketch, bent the fire, tugged at each one's emotions differently.

"I want to go the baths," Blade whined, eager to meet men and ashamed at the same time.

Heather May touched his cheek reassuringly. Her bracelets dangled and banged against each other. Burnished by firelight, transformed by sun, her formerly pale face was set with eyes like sapphire stones or twinkling stars. For a moment, she lit the night.

A stick, now ignited, spit sparks. Harry passed around pewter bowls of beans. Jinx, blithe, lightly aided him, handed out spoons and cloth of some kind, for napkins. She broke open her gathered cloth bag, extracting three dark loaves. Seeds sparkled out on the pumpernickel and black backdrop. Each one was passed as ceremoniously as the wine that followed—wine dark red, almost crimson like Jinx's pants. Each bite smelled like fire smoke. I was eating sputtering wood, swallowing molten amber and wine-hued fire.

Blade looked nervous, preoccupied. He wanted to go to the baths. A fat, long number was passed, weed dripping out of it like verdant sperm.

"I pass," I said. The others took their fill. We wove through the dark by Harry's light, into his dark dusty Scout and drove by spinney headlights that lit the spongy little plants we'd passed earlier into fluttering glow of ice plants and fox breath and heather.

Barreling down the short steep mountain road we rumbled and braked and fell until we reached the gate leading off Harry's land to the main highway. Heather May and Leon held tight to each other in the back next to me. Blade and Harry and Jinx were squeezed together up front.

Harry took off hard onto the main highway. Though fast drivers, neither he nor Frannie Jinx Smythe could live up to the legend of her race car father. Harry projected us toward the baths. When we slowed near Esalen, I relaxed. By now I knew the routine.

When the big names in therapy, Fritz Perls and the others, had conferences at Esalen, their folks stayed in cabins. Later in the evening, the beats and hippies slipped in and enjoyed among the shadows path and enjoyed the mysticism of the moment. Tonight our group slipped down the moonlit silver pathway through the catacombs and into the water—five bodies splashing playfully. The paying guests had gone.

Blade held back, but Heather May pulled him in. He only giggled at her nudity, he was her trusted friend. The golden shape of a nude, slight young man flitted by us like a white shade, toward to the south wall and into his own tub.

"Blade's gonna find a girl one of these days, isn't he, Leon?" Heather May comforted Blade, who emanated humiliation from his dark corner.

Compulsively honest as they'd said—Jinx rose from the water. "Come on, Blade," she invited, incredulous that he wasn't like the rest of us. "You mean you don't like women? You're afraid, that's all."

I admired Jinx's whole persona. Steamy glasses under dark hair, beautiful muscled, boys back and arms, two taut nipples pointed forward from small breasts, one even smaller than the other.

She leaned across Harry and passed yet another joint. I watched her with the eye of an artist. I wanted to get the look of that arm extended with its full muscle and the cleavage of chest turning into breasts. She was easy to sketch while in motion, harder for me to draw from recall.

After everyone except me took a hit, Blade stretched out his long arms, white at the forearms, around Heather May and Leon. A squiggle of "whose toes?" in the dark water in response.

The rainbow nimbus around the slim moon increased. What would it be like tomorrow?

I stood up—too hot! Paul Beannie followed me as he always did. Slightly shorter than I, older, unemployed, weak, kindly, he was a sycophant. He fished another joint from his parka, pursed his lips and asked, "You wanna try it–once?"

Crisp with fear and the ocean foggy air, I drew away. Paul Beannie well knew I was afraid because of my bad experiences in Berkeley, Mexico with Kesey, and another time when I'd met him at Big Sur. I was so afraid of all that stuff I was even angry.

"I'm angry, man." I squared my shoulders and feet. "I'm angry at that because you know how I feel."

Blade, Heather May, Leon, Jinx and Harry murmured convivially in the tub. At half past three they'd respectively "dropped" acid.

"Hold on," Heathie blurted.

A heavy loquacious silence crept over them, electric and profound. It all terrified me—their stuff, smoking opium, chewing mushrooms, hasheesh brownies, speed and even grass and the garden seeds my neighbor Mak and I had chewed. I became irrationally afraid of the water.

In my non-drugged state I imagined "it"—whatever it was—in the water, and the ones who had taken "it" as thin–membraned creatures from which "it" oozed.

I was grateful Paul Beannie had refrained from acid tonight–for me–but he had toked deep and long, though.

Cool foggy mists touched my bare back, but it was an ambivalent pleasure, reminding me of a night in the Haight at Gene's drug dealer friends' Ceasar's house. I'd awakened to trippy Pennie and her crazy friend Hatch wrapping me in Saran Wrap while I'd lain sleeping nude.

The creativity, sexuality, was a welcome balm, but the drugs were the shadow that had ruined it all for me. Even though I wanted to be with them this morning, in the bath.

Wet, fresh-scented air rose from waves surging and throttling the beach. Cleansing. For the first time I thought, I wasn't really that afraid; and Paul was here.

I dove back into the water, sitting a little away from the others and feeling left out that I couldn't join them in altering their minds. Mine was sensitive enough without anything.

Just before the dawn they rose up one by one and I followed. They were going up on the lawn to see the rising of the spring equinox, Easter sun. Paul and I reached the rise before the others who were slowed by their "trips" and wondering at any little marvelous thing.

"See this tiny red living little brother," Leon exclaimed at a microscopic — I couldn't see it — insect, winding up and down the wooden railing above the sea. "He too is a part of it."

"Oh, Leon," Heather May whispered.

Paul and I stood together watching the moon, which, to his bleary eyes, was "far out". Again he offered me a toke, honestly eager for me to belong to the beauty.

I looked up, wanting to see beauty, to "pass the test" somehow like them, and in one instant be enlightened, like the hollow unsound inside the Zen parables in Leon's book. To this end I toked — once, twice, even a third time. Afterwards I stared down at my knees, giving in at last to terror.

Paul nudged. I looked up.

Then I saw it, the glimmering of the rings of the moon. There had been one, now there were too.

I steadied myself on the railing. I was suddenly outbound and saw the beautiful sea of just-before-dawn opalescent clouds combed into careful rows like the fast- passing Brussel sprouts and artichokes fields on the way past Watsonville to Monterey.

White waves swept from the upper right of the horizon down, combed across the still-wintry, ringed moon like silt sifted across a golden nugget. They made an opening, a cache for the deep resonant moon, whose three rings glistened and shone like the far-away rings of Saturn turned to more fortunate Jupiter.

"Paul," I uttered, a part of me still deeply afraid of altering my mind in any way. I clutched his sleeve, "Paul, it is beautiful."

He smiled in lackadaisical approbation. He had accomplished something. Now we were one.

After the sun had risen, we followed the others, up—out of the baths, up the narrow pathway leading above the sea to the great, dew-wet lawns that curled around the shallow, distressed-wood buildings. An iron, latticed, low railing framed the lawn—only a token barrier, above the hard drop down.

On this dawn, this Easter equinox dawn, the lawn, when I looked down, was a jewel, a blink of the eye tone of red—not green—under the rising light. And the copper iron fence glinted blue, not burnished, beneath the reflections of the barely blurring skyline.

I looked around at everyone's faces. It seemed they'd seen it too—this lovely dazzle of opposite fluorescent sheens of colors mirrored by the magic of an inner, undiscovered mind. How beautiful.

And I'd passed. I'd never take this stuff again.

Chapter 17

San Francisco

Weeks later, after a party at Olive's San Francisco Art Institute, A. Chase Streeter draped his long legs and huge, incandescent, uncircumcised penis across my thigh. It felt light in his dark apartment.

He lit a cigarette. It was cold, with a draft under the door and the big high-unheated ceilings. Way outside his flat, the ring of the cable car clanging up Hyde Street.

After sex for some reason, I was afraid, being with him. Heir to the Manhatten Bank, brother a curator of the Boston Art Museum... It wasn't that, though—I was an heir to something, to something much bigger. I could feel it. No, this was different. Something special.

I leaned into him. Wished I could talk, but my feet were cold. Actually I'd been cold a lot lately, shaky, trying to go to school, classes of a thousand, and the small, advanced standing English tutorial. It was hard to listen about the literature I loved and stay composed and answer and stuff, because I could barely stay in my seat.

Like tonight, I couldn't tell anyone there about the fear, the freezing hands, the feeling I was distant from my body.

Music from Chase's "found art" cabinet moved in and around us in the dark. Beautiful, supple sounds, like our limbs, strange, long, sinewy. He was the second son trying to make a name for himself as an artist and by decorating and furnishing his place only with found things.

After my first time with him, when I'd gone back to school in Berkeley from his house in the city, I'd left a poem for him on scraps of paper. He made fun of me, writing mocking renditions of my poems on humiliating post cards, sending them to me in Berkeley. Days later, he'd followed me over to my co-ed, redwood-shingled rooming house over on the bus. I forgot I was humiliated, because, kind enough to know he was wrong to mock me, he said I was a beautiful, earnest girl.

Now, at the end of my time with him, I stayed at his new place—higher ceilings, scary to me somehow, or was it because I was nervous, since I'd taken to hitching everywhere? Tomorrow I'd leave from the Oak Street off ramp near his house, down to Big Sur.

He played the song about how we are but a moment's sunlight fading in the grass. Magnificent jewels of rain pelted the house, and I thought we were mere shadows, unfilled forms, waiting for the substance of the people we would become, and waiting for the people we would one-day love.

"You do everything right," he said, "but at the wrong time."

He looked at me quizzically. "When you're older...you'll be OK. You'll be great."

He looked pleased with himself to make such pronouncements, like he was more than the third heir to Manhatten, like he was the one who'd made it all the way. From the first night, he'd been working on a painting of my long body like a fish in his bath, for the Art Institute display. Olive later said he redid it and redid it. Maybe it hangs somewhere today, and maybe he looks at it and remembers lying, sleeping uneasily on white sheets over bare mattress with a single clock marking time above a photograph of the Manhatten clan before a whitewashed Cape Cod house.

I wondered at the time, if being a Manhattenite wouldn't have been a resting-place, finally thought, no, because I couldn't talk when he was sorting out what worked in me and what had to go. I'll bet he even painted over my mons veneris and made an aquamarine smudge. I was a "found art" piece to him, too big to fit in.

In the morning, I headed out toward the white, glimmering, rain-fresh street. I gave him one sweet kiss and didn't leave a poem. And he didn't advise me as to my youthful mistiming, but he looked sad.

The song about the evening of the day, watching children play, "smiling faces I can see—but not for me," played on his clock radio, played through the great bay window while I left.

I never saw him again, but neither forgot. Somewhere a man I might still be interested in, presides over curios in the Boston museum. A picture of a nude Berkeley girl painted in 1967 hangs untitled in a back room, a momento to compensate for chic evenings of coke and Brie with current museum friends.

"Hard to meet anyone when you're young and try out your life on them," he would say now if he said anything at all about the subject of the painting, whose blued-over mons veneris he would—with greater wisdom—have left just the way it was.

Woodside, California

I had hitched from Oak Street to Big Sur and back up the peninsula again, then to Berkeley, where I'd met Jinx and an effete millionaire Stanford harpsichordist, Edward Fayette Worthington and his fellow philosophy friend Hans. The four of us stayed up, nude all weekend, Jinx and I sketching by candlelight. Parting and absorbing for a week after, we could all feel it. Jinx went over to Hans and Edward met me in Palo Alto, swept me to his rented hilltop chalet. I felt bad because she'd met him first, but "the embrace doesn't lie," she said. It didn't. That led me to break it off with Paul completely and move in between terms with Edward in Woodside.

What peace to be at Edward's after a series of fleeting encounters, from the Esalen Baths to the Art Institute. To be nurtured as a creative individual instead of just screwed as nameless Girl, too young and too numb to want the pummeling she would relish in maturity.

We talked in front of Edward's Woodside fireplace. About his life growing up in Idaho, father became a millionaire when others went to war, his potato farms fed the troops. Talented, too close to his mother, Edward lived on his father's allowance, was well liked by many, including the Hemingway granddaughters and Hunter S. Thompson.

Soft white gold flames rose up the two sides of the logs. For me, the shadow of chaotic experiences gave way to love.

After the fire grew low, we lay in his A-frame living room on a mattress and springs covered by sheets. He'd let the Bach Cello Suites Numbers Two and Three, wind down. The needle lingered in the empty band beyond sound. The evenly balanced, high-pitched speakers sang out jewel toned thrusts of dust mote notes against the needle on the high-priced, whining turntable.

Edward returned to the bed in the high-vaulted room; a great glass window beyond the baby grand piano, framed a view of jutting timber, miles and miles down toward the golden gate.

125

He pulled off short boots. I'd never seen boots like these. He put aside his crisp, starched shirt and lay beside me. Although he was a handsome man, large blue eyes, snowy blond hair, strong back, in the firelight, his back appeared bent, his high domed head, a monstrosity.

Cold, I folded back into the bed, propped up on my elbow. I jackknifed into his cool, clean sheets, much more afraid than at sixteen with Nors in Manzanillo, or at Paul Beannie's first grope on New Year's Eve at the roach-infested Kensington Hotel.

Here was a man balding, plain in the distorted light, mal-formed. I read his features through fear and the Scotch he'd given me. He too had had a bad drug experience and though barely 23 himself, he understood and comforted me. He rose over me in the dark.

He twisted in his private, removed, hot, way, around in his own recessed fantasies, until we were in position.

Afterwards, he muttered, "Why not, we're both middle class," and then I caught that word—marriage. I thought we were in business; that's how it was going to be. It was a wisp of a dream, like a harpsichord fugue, a dust mote on record, or Scotch preserved.

I'd found an opening, a cache of tenderness and pity in this man.

The next day, as dizzy as the bride I hoped to be, I attempted to do the dishes when he asked me to—the first time in my life. Away from the bed, he was cool and reserved. By the time I'd gotten to the sink I'd lost the security I'd felt at midnight. I didn't want him to think I would have done anything to please him, even though I would have. Unlocked by loving him all at once, I plied myself to do right and impress him, but somehow still acted like an ignoble, sullen eighteen-year-old.

Masking ignorance at how to help, I looked out the empty, cold, curtainless windows, past garbage cans to the forest. A squeeze of stupid thoughts ran like squirrels in a hoop.

I wanted free from these last years of fear and denied dependency, feeling like yesterday's garbage. I wanted free of the days before, and the days before that. Would the gate, opened, shut back upon itself?

As I looked at him, I knew my eyes were glittering with intense connection. But the net was that I acted eighteen, an extremist. After dinner he played for me on his grand piano. I spun around to refill his drink and knocked over a lamp. But at night I wound my body around him, like long hair intertwined with the leather fringe of my lost jacket.

I pressed to his skin, my cheek to his shoulder, while we slept. He seemed to accept me doing that. Even though I knew I had to go back to Berkeley, I rested for the first time in many years.

A bit of log fell. Flames, blue and white gold, leapt up like long hair suddenly shaken free. I nestled deeper into the safe cache of love, and dreamed.

Turning in the dark to see the fire later, I saw the flames dancing like sea foam, splattering behind dark rocks lumbering in the foreground just before the break of quiet on a predawn beach.

Chapter 18

Berkeley

"You can't come in here," a neat, madras-clad girl shouted above me.

"I can go anywhere I want," I yelled back, too absorbed in what I was writing to look up.

Grabbing my poetry notebook, I sidestepped the gate, climbed through trash and flowers and stepped up the alley between the Kappa Sorority and the University of California campus. It was 1968 now. I had just arrived in Berkeley to attend my next term. It was not the first time. I was born here, then often returned here between that time and today.

"She looks haggard." The sorority girls tittered in the window above me. "Like a dirty hippie."

I didn't care.
I had things to do.
I would do them.

After words

Dear Lynn,

I've finally finished reading your very fine book. No doubt about it, you are a very talented writer as well as a natural born artist. I'm deeply impressed.

I think the book is an important contribution to our knowledge of the sixties. The reader is allowed to observe the sixties' failed revolution through the very perceptive, aware, intelligent, female, teenaged eyes (about whom it revolved and from whom it emanated) an age that almost but not quite changed the world forever. (If only!) All you need is love.....

This talented teenager, whose honest, forthright stance, daring attitude and bold, impassioned gestures are so characteristic of her generation, speaks of her generation's faith in the Universe and its wondrous possibilities. She never questions her own validity. Her innocence and unquestioned sense of self-worth were always astonishing to someone from an earlier generation who never felt innocent but vaguely guilty of unspecified but self-evident through unrealized, sinful cravings. ("Shall I wear my stockings rolled? Should I eat a peach?" makes me think I was not the only one suffering from such doubts and that it was a generation's malaise rather than just a co-dependent characteristic.) You were very brave, daring and perceptive.

If I've ever felt the "warm attention of sailors" I'd never had such words to even think about it, for example.

Chapter eleven was great!

Fabulous descriptions of Ken K. and Mt. Girl in Chapter 12. On page 88, I would have said, "that night the women except Mt. Girl (who never went near a kitchen in my experience) washed the dishes....."

I loved Acapulco and Curlee and McGee and their imagined sexuality. (Funny, my experience of Acapulco, a few years later, was something like yours in Puerto Vallarta. I was walking on the beach in front of the big, luxurious hotels. There on the rocks I saw a baby—all alone. As I got closer I saw that it was lying in a pool of shit—dysentery. But I could feel hidden eyes on me and knew better than to touch the poor child, who was still alive and needed to go to a hospital. So I just went on. It was ghastly.)

Why not call the book Growing Up in the Sixties?

Thank you for the opportunity of reading this book. I almost want to copy it for my granddaughter, who is 18 and wants to be a writer, but so sheltered by Catholic schools and protected from these fearful and fearsome 80's and 90's. Instead, though, I'll wait until the book is published, which I'm sure it will be.

Best of luck. You really are a wonderful writer Lynn.

Ann Marie Maxwell
Beat Artist

Mexican Lament

Silky
Long hair drips across
La musica triste
"Pues yo soy como el chile verde"
El llamo, the cry, begins
Slick white teeth; pink bouffant lips
Bleat
A piquant, latino beat
Reminds me

Of a Mexican night 1966
In a courtyard caliente
Putas, whores, gather at the far end
Of a courtyard caliente
And I, the only little girl with Nietsche
Fat, softbound
Squeezed between her sweaty palms,
Called abuelita (I was not that blonde)
Sat one night in the bar
At diez y sies anos
Sixteen, sola, alone
In a place
Where chile pepper colored cactus
Popped through tamale sands
And the night sky crackled
As crabs scuttled across
Pebble dry black sand troughs
To the sea
(All black things to the sea)
The putas coagulated at the far end of the
Motel it seemed to me
"Puta," I asked one of these
In the crackling hot pork skin night
"Porque se trabajas asi?

Digame: Lucha para las mujeres and all,"
I recall I said
"Get out of here kid."
They recognized me for what I was:
A deterrent to business
A Nietsche-loving Northamerican kid
Oh I didn't know that "Ubermensch"
That Supermensch
Meant only mensch

Not yet, not then
Come back, mujeres
Back to la madre the sea I said
How was I to know I offered them only salt
In Nietsche: I later read
He hitched
A woman writer for a picture
To a dogcart in a ditch
So she could drag
His silly friend and him
By silver cords through dirt

Silken tendrils: long hair drips
Across la musica triste
There is no hope in this
But out there in the crackling night
There was

In here you were only
Brujas: witches
Only
The mirror
Of some man's desire to
Incinerate
The bruja
Within
His own

Soul the yin
Be whole
Come read
Nietsche
On the road
With the
Crabs
And me
Please
Por favor
(Please)

I offer you an imperfect
Conoscimiento
Though one of hope
By one candle's light
A rivuleted sand trough cheek
Mujer muy viejo/woman very old
Pats a tortilla
In the vocabulary of the voiceless dark:
Old, old soul, bruja, puta
Her hands pronounce.
And your girlchildren,
Who play outside
Hear the wild cold notes of the mariache
Boring through supple courtyard walls;
His beachcracked lips
Blow his trembling trombone
Like a bone.
Pit pat the tortilla slaps
The children's rubbertire guaraches
Flap over broken, steppingstone tile
They pile outside
And work the quesadilla oily doorknobs to get in
Don't let them;
Come to the sea with me
Let's splash

In scalding spray
Wring your bodies
Inside out
And rumpled lay them
On charcoal sand
By boiling sea
Come out
A thousand silver starfish
Will quiver echolalicly
As the abandoned mariache
Beats his pastiche
Into the empty cots and florid walls
Of your burlap blanket prison stalls.

All the yin in the world
On the head of a pin
Is not the yin
That there is yin is sure
That it is purely intuition
Revives
The treatise Mary Wollstonecraft denied:
How did he put it, that one, last, fumbling sot?
That mumbling minister, lay organ of the dictum of his day?
Why, "woman reasons not," his hot breath blew
Out at the congregation

"Not this" dear putas, dear brujas, she cried
Line up quickly in a row
Keep your eyes on Mary as you go
Pick your way through the starfish and the noodle-ey roe
Refrain from singing with the
Mariache, whose siren hands on the dying wind/
Pues yo soy como el chile verde
Llorona,
Llorona,
Piquante pero sabroso--
Go quickly.

Olive speaks

Colly Ryder was the original hippy. Before the word "hippy" was coined. Colly discarded conventions right and left, leaving them scattered behind her, like Heidi's winter clothes. Fascinated but unable to keep up with her, I watched in amazement as my disreputable friend zoomed through my life, vanished, resurfaced and vanished again.

Colly arrived at Pacific High School in the middle of her sophomore year. Quiet and expressionless, this carefully groomed girl in her tidy public school clothes looked conventional and dull. But on a school camping trip we struck up a conversation, and I was taken by Colly's brilliance and originality. We became close friends immediately. The facade fell away. Colly had been trying to impress the administration of our small private school, disguising herself as a "good girl". She'd recently been busted in a house with jazz musicians, and was accepted at Pacific High on a trial basis.

I was to graduate before Colly. I spent a year in Berkeley, fervently working for Jerry Rubin's Viet Nam Day Committee, then four years in San Francisco as an art student. This was a time of struggle for me. Young for my age, the big world was too cold, difficult to navigate, hard to understand. I remember Colly's periodic visits with pleasure and some anger as well. A speck would appear in the sky. I watched anxiously as the long awaited visitor, the rare and exoitc bird approached, grew larger, circled and landed, resplendent with colorful feathers and sometimes accompanied by an entourage.

The entourage was Berkeley brownshingle I had recently moved into, my new roommates were not amused. But on other visits, Colly and I explored the city together, shared adventures, talked until dawn. "Come to bed!" my boyfriend hollered from the other room of our tiny North Beach apartment. Jealous of my time, he thought I should "outgrow my high school friends."

Colly was the original hippy. But in the end she was not a hippy at all. Too smart, too verbal, too analytical to flourish in an anti-intellectual subculture. Colly was too intelligent to mouth platitudes, too complicated to be "mellow" or "just flow".

I graduated from art school and my friend Colly moved off in another direction and dropped out of my life. I inherited some money, bought a Volkswagen, and with enormous exhilaration and relief fled the city and embarked on my own odyssey across the United States. I was to settle in a rural community, becoming a new kind of hippy, a "back to the land" hippy, passionately growing fruits and vegetables, enjoying brilliant blue skies and starry nights. I stayed there twenty years.

Once on a visit home, I saw Colly in her suburban house in San Jose. I was struck by the stark decor. She had two little girls and a husband. She told me she'd joined some kind of metaphysical group. I didn't get it, which surprised me as she'd been this hippy with flair. But that was part of her personality too, the ability to go in and out of roles.

That was decades ago. Last year we reconnected with amazing ease. The facades of "hippy" and "straight person" have dropped away. But Colly and Olive are still there, adults now, artists and writers, able to navigate through the world without crashing into things, causing havoc, but basically the same two people. "It's like we're teenagers in a play," Colly says, "the same, with a few silver streaks painted on," and I think this must be true.

Author's Notes

Born in Berkeley is the memoir of a pivotal period in the mid 1960's. Although written as fiction, the facts are true. After the Beats and before the Hippies were named, many neighborhoods like "Tupper's Park" sprang up on the San Francisco Bay peninsula.

The term Beat came from the New Testament Beatitudes, which spoke of living simply. "The meek shall inherit the earth." Beaten down by materialistic white American culture of the forties and early fifties, Beat outsiders wrote poetry to the beat of Negro hipsters' music.

Meanwhile, mainstream World War Two couples--raised in the Great Depression--bestowed attention and advantages on their postwar offspring. Gave their kids a lot. Patriotic ideas and the leisure to question the fifties emphasis on conformity. Look alike houses covered up shameful social problems. The cultural pendulum had swung too far.

A small percentage of youth born in this suburban security, threw off their advantages and privilege. Very like the youth of twelfth century Assisi, Italy, following Sts. Francis and Clare, after whom San Francisco and Santa Clara are named. The Assisi youth tossed away their parents' cloth of gold, cut their hair in this case, and took to the road, following Christ's Beat message.

Like these, Caroline Ryder in <u>Born In Berkeley</u> was ostracized by her peers who today try to claim the Summer of Love as their own.

But by 1967, the real sixties mavericks had done their work. Their civil rights, peace and free speech marches had broken ground for Be-Ins and Grateful Dead music. Now even the "popular kids" who had ridiculed their few long haired classmates, came to Haight and Ashbury Streets in San Francisco, put on love beads for an hour on the weekend. The commercialized hippie was in vogue.

But it is to the small group of sixties youth who first gave up privilege and followed that beat to the heart of a new--and timeless--life, to whom this book is dedicated.